How Many Hills to Hillsboro?

how many hills to hillsboro?
by fred bauer

HEWITT HOUSE

Old Tappan, New Jersey

For Shirley,
who overlooks
and understands

Preface

For a good many people, this is a story which needs no introduction whatsoever. They know the Bauer family of Princeton, New Jersey, already. By *they*, we mean the millions of folks who learned about these adventuresome bicyclers while they were still on their ten-week cross-country trip last summer. In most cases, it was an introduction brought about by a newspaper story, a television newscast or radio interview. However, for many, many others, it was a firsthand meeting. Some vacationers stopped their cars along the road to chat, others met them at campsites as they pitched their tent, still others at roadside tables, swimming pools, restaurants, parks, etc. . . . To all of these people, this story—a love story with America—will hold extra special meaning.

To those who don't know the Bauers, let us give you a quick summary. They left on their bicycling-camping vacation from New York City, June 7. The participants were writer and editor thirty-four-year-old Fred Bauer, who narrates the trip in this book; Shirley Bauer, thirty-two, his wife and the mother of their three children; Laraine, thirteen; Steve, eleven; and Christopher, three, who made the ride on a special seat on the back of Daddy's bike. Why the Bauers made the trip and what they discovered about America, Americans and themselves is the theme of this book.

If with that background, your soul is stirred with unfulfilled wanderlust, grab your bike and come along. It will be a ride you won't soon forget.

The Publishers

Table of Contents

How Many Hills to Hillsboro?

1 Shades of Kermit the Creep

"I can't go on," puffed Steve, out of breath.

As I turned toward him, I saw a rivulet of sweat run a course his frown had made, off his grease-smudged forehead and down a sun-reddened cheek. He brushed it away and then put his fist to one eye to dam up an imminent storm.

I understood, for I was so exhausted myself that I easily could have joined him in a good cry. Yet I knew we had at least another hour's climb before we reached the summit and a site we hoped would be suitable for pitching a tent.

By we, I mean my wife Shirley, who at thirty-two is two years my junior; Laraine, thirteen, Steve, eleven, and Christopher, three. The five of us were at this moment on a cross-country bicycle trip, a little more than two hundred miles from our starting point, New York City's Battery Park, just north of the Statue of Liberty.

We thought Miss Liberty an appropriate launching point, considering we were going to try to ride our four bicycles (Christopher had a special seat on the back of mine) all the way across America, finishing at Los Angeles and the Pacific.

Before one assumes that I am a former Olympic decathlon performer or that my wife is some sort of Amazon, let me interject that we were about as surprised to be making the trip as most people who heard about it. I had not ridden a bicycle farther than "around the block" since I was a boy. Where I grew up in Ohio anyone over twenty-one who persisted in pedaling about on a two-wheeler was considered to have a serious problem. And in some cases, it was true. A fellow we called among ourselves Kermit the Creep, an obese bachelor of thirty-five or forty, I suppose, used to ride up and down the streets of our neighborhood clad in a brilliant orange striped silk jacket. Though we would call the jacket a good safety measure today, Kermit was not aware of it. He thought it tasteful. On his head he wore a forerunner of the modern racing helmet, but his gear was a closer facsimile of the helmet Red Grange wore to fame, galloping ghost-like across the gridirons of the Big Ten. Around both pantlegs, Kermit clamped wires to keep his trousers out

of the chain. All of this, set in motion, made an unforgettable billowing sight which quickly popped into
my mind when we first talked of a bicycle trip.

But that was months earlier. At the moment, the bicycling Bauer family was struggling up one of the Pennsylvania mountains, on the other side of Chambersburg.
We had started our ascent about three o'clock that afternoon and by six o'clock we were about three-fourths of
the way up. With the exception of the first fifty yards,
which we all managed to pedal, Shirley, Steve and I had
walked our bikes. Laraine—she has the intestinal grit of
her Grandmother Juna—struggled on, making short
thrusts of thirty-five or forty yards before she draped
over the handlebars, out of wind.

When we began the climb, the sun at our left was
bearing down unmercifully and we kept dragging on the
two canteens until our water supply ebbed dangerously
low. But by six o'clock the tree line shadows had become
friends and journeyed over to our side of the road to walk
with us up the hill. The humidity also came along, however.

Now pushing a bicycle, the kind known in the trade
as a lightweight, about thirty pounds stripped, may not
seem a back-breaking ordeal to most, but let me explain.
To the thirty pounds of each bicycle, we had added steel
baskets front and back, a sixteen-pound tent, five sleeping
bags, a camp stove, rain gear, two changes of clothing
for everyone, minimum food, spare bike parts and tools
and other paraphernalia peculiar to campers. In addition,
my bike was equipped with a special seat for forty-pound

Christopher, who sat astride the back fender, nonchalantly playing with toy cars while I struggled forward. My bike, with Christopher, carried about sixty-five pounds additional weight, while Shirley was saddled with an extra thirty-five and Laraine and Steve with about twenty-five pounds each.

So when Steve called out in desperation, "I can't go on," I was in great sympathy with him.

"Let's try to make it up to that opening," I said, pointing to the next curve where the shoulder widened on our side. He said he would try and after two or three bursts followed by brief breath-catchers, we made it. There, we parked our bikes against the cable that stood between us and a seventy-five-foot drop, and we sat down to rest. A hundred yards below, I could see Shirley and Laraine leaning over their handlebars, trying to catch their breath.

We had both canteens with us, so they had no water and it would take them another ten minutes to get to us. I thought of going down to them, but decided instead that I would go without water until they reached us. That seemed to be a good compromise. But Steve and Chris both took careful sips before the canteen was returned to Steve's front basket.

I leaned back against the cable and closed my eyes. Dr. Norman Vincent Peale once told me that when he gets hot and bothered, he finds it helpful to think of the most tranquil scene he can remember. I tried to recall the coolest places I'd ever been. The picture that came to mind was of the beach at Nice on the Riviera. We had gone there on a family vacation the summer before, camping on that trip, too, but we did it more conventionally—by car.

The picture of myself lolling in the sand under a huge umbrella, being fanned by a gentle sea breeze, lasted all of twenty seconds. It was Shirley's voice which brought me out of my reverie.

"Laraine's got a flat tire," she called from below, about seventy-five yards now.

"Good grief," I said, "whose bright idea was it to try this stunt anyway."

"Yeah, whose?" said Steve with a smirk.

2 Around Cape Horn

It had all begun three months earlier.

Outside, the raw March wind had the bare arms of our front-yard maple swinging like a symphony orchestra conductor gone mad. Inside, logs diced from a brother maple which failed to survive the previous summer harvest served as a stage for dancing, singing flames.

But for me, the wind was not a suburban New Jersey blow. No, it was a foul northeaster ripping at the sails of my ship, fighting its way around Cape Horn; and the brattle coming from the fireplace was creaking timbers of the deck. Both were excellent sound effects for the script which I held (or held me) against the soft arm of the sofa. Sir Francis Chichester was telling the story of his solo odyssey around the world with the *Gypsy Moth*. In my mind, I was right there with the good skipper (or good writer, for I wouldn't know a good sailor from a lousy one) with each wave's rise and fall. Ready to run to his aid, to lend a hand with the jib or the boom or with whatever it is one lends a hand. Only the voice of the navigator of my house saying that she was going topside—ah, upstairs—to bed was able to wrest me from being inundated by a sixty-five-foot monster wave.

I closed the book and followed Shirley up the stairs, still bubbling with vicarious excitement. She was unmoved by my story recreation, probably because she becomes seasick just thinking about the sea. Once she got woozy watching a fresh bar of Ivory bob in her bath. And there had been the rough crossing following our Hawaiian departure: Shirley tossed her lei overboard and then watched to see if it would return to shore. Tradition says if the flowers do, you will return to the Islands someday. Strange, but she stood railside for three days claiming to be looking after her wreath.

"Wouldn't that be some experience," I enthused. "Sailing around the world."

She had already disappeared beneath the covers and was not about to be locked into a sleep-detaining dialogue.

"Wouldn't it be fun to go on some such way out adventure?" I tried again.

Silence.

"I don't mean sailing around the world, but say hiking from the East to West coast. Taking the out-of-the-way routes. That would be a fascinating way to really discover America, wouldn't it?"

"Go to sleep," she finally commanded, making one of those fast rolls which left me with nothing but a camel-looking hump with which to converse. It didn't stop me.

"If not coast-to-coast on foot, Shirley, maybe on bike. Now that wouldn't be out of the question. We could take the summer. Camp. Sight-see. I could do some interviews. Some writing. You know when I was a boy, a gang of us was going to take a Model A cross-country, but it fell through because. . . ."

The form beside me, I observed, had lapsed into one of those deep, undulating breathing patterns that told me, unequivocally, I had lost my audience. I cocked my arm as if to smack that camel hump, but then I stopped short. Do you suppose, I wondered, that anyone has ever ridden across the U.S. on a camel?

The next morning on my way to the kitchen, the sight of the Chichester book set me off again.

"What about a camping trip across the country this summer?" I began. "We could take a couple of months. Do it nice and easy this time."

"Swell," Shirley answered, buttering her toast. "Better get new tires on the wagon."

"No, I was thinking we might travel by bike."

"You're fevered. Drink your orange juice," she raised her eyebrows toward the ceiling and her eyes followed them up. "When are you going to call the plumber? That pipe's been leaking again."

But I wasn't licked. That evening I stopped off at the public library and researched the subject. Among other things, I learned that the cross-country record for riding a bike was twenty-seven days. It was set in 1940 by a rider who had pedaled from New York to San Francisco. Furthermore, I discovered that Dr. Paul Dudley White, the Boston heart specialist who attended President Eisenhower, is an avid cyclist himself and a strong proponent of the sport for its exercise value.

"Maybe I should switch to cycling," I told Shirley that evening. For nearly six months, I had been on a jogging kick, running a half mile each morning before breakfast.

"It might be safer," she answered. "One of these days that Great Dane is going to catch you." By way of explaining that one: anyone who jogs around his neighborhood knows that dogs don't care much for cantering men in baggy sweatshirts and clapping sneakers. Furthermore, I suspect some of their masters don't care much for joggers, either. I had caught a number of people peeking from behind shades and curtains, suspiciously observing me on the trot. Though it never happened, I thoroughly expected a police officer to come to my door some evening and ask me to explain my behavior. "You were seen running away from the Wagners this morning," I imagined him to say. "Now, this is no accusation, but the Wagners have reported their power mower missing. You wouldn't know anything about it?"

"Well," I continued in my conversation with Shirley, "tomorrow is my thirty-fourth birthday, and I am going to buy myself a present, a bicycle."

"I need a new one, too," said Laraine, looking up from the homework she was sharing with television.

"Good," I said, "I'll buy everyone a new bike, if you all promise to get up mornings and go riding with me." For the first time, Shirley's eyes warmed. It was her maternal warmth.

"The whole family go riding every morning. . . ." Her voice trailed off into head-nodding assent. "Yes, I think that might be a good idea." I left her muttering something about family togetherness.

The next afternoon, Shirley and I went shopping for my birthday present—in quadruplicate.

3 Gee, Dad, It's a Schwinn!

"I'd like to buy a bicycle," I said somewhat self-consciously to the salesman in the first store we visited.

"For yourself?" he asked. I listened carefully for some hint of cynicism, some sarcastic inflection, but there was none. Only another question: What type of bicycle? I hesitated. Was he putting me on? What kinds are there? One with crossbars for boys and without bars for girls; English lightweights and Americans with the heavy frames and balloon tires—at least those were the choices the last time I bought a bike.

"Well, how do you plan to use your bicycle?" he continued. Now that was a honey of a question too. I thought of telling him my name was Wright, Orville Wright, and that I had this crazy brother at home who had an idea that if we took a bike apart and used the chain and pedals on a gizmo with wings we could fly like birds. Instead, I rubbed my chin and looked at the floor.

"Well . . . I thought . . . we thought. . . ." I motioned toward Shirley, who stood there amusedly watching her Mr. Confidence in pain. "We thought we might like a couple of bikes to ride around town for exercise . . . or maybe on short trips . . . say a day or two with camping equipment . . . or we might even take them on our vacation this summer."

For a minute, the man just stared at me. Then—mercifully—he invited us into the throne room where thousands, well, maybe hundreds, of glistening bicycles in a myriad of colors stood before us. My first revelation was that bicycles have paint and two pedals. The first bike I owned had neither. It also was minus a front fender and had only a trace of tin over the back tire, or what was once a tire. The rear tire of that bike had more patches than one of Grandma Strayer's prized quilts, and it needed resuscitation once a day at the gas station. Otherwise, the bike was in perfect condition, save for the chain which kept slipping, a faulty coaster brake and handlebars with spent threads.

What an adventure it was pedaling papers with those rotating handlebars. At least once a night, they gave way and I went crashing down on the basket. "Look Mom, no hands . . . no teeth!" I never understood how I got such a gypping on that bike, considering I paid a whole nine dollars for it.

"Now, we have bikes for every age, every purpose and in every price range," said the salesman, leading us first past a group of featherlight, stripped-down models that reminded me of my old wreck. The handlebars had fallen down near the pedals the same way, though these were shaped differently, like handlebar moustaches. (I wonder: Were handlebars named after the moustache or the moustache after the handlebars?) There were some differences, however. Most noticeably the price tag: $195.

"These bikes are fifteen-speed," continued the man. "They're racing bikes." I studied the intricate mechanism: five different sprockets surrounded the back axle and up front were three more. Apparently, bike racers don't take any chances with losing out because of a broken sprocket, I thought. I asked how these busy-looking gears worked and he began by pointing to what he called a *dérailleur*. I didn't have any such apparatus when I was delivering papers, my chain derailed quite nicely by itself.

"When you're going uphill," he went on, "you can ease your pedal work by shifting gears with this stick up here." Up by the handlebars he pointed to a steel lever which tightened or loosened a cable connected to this *dérailleur* business.

After the fifteen-speed, he showed me ten- and five- and three- and ungeared bikes—my old friend at last. Prices ranged from $29.95 for a Japanese model called a Tinfin,

I believe, to the $250 racing bikes from Italy. I don't remember the latter's name: *Amore* or something sexy.

In the end, I thanked the man for his time and told him I would no doubt be back when I made up my mind . . . "and providing Dad gives me the money," I whispered to Shirley.

Outside, she tried to lead me into Fifi's French Fashions where in the window she had spotted a svelte-looking green sheath draped over a facsimile of Gina Lollobrigida.

"If you want pedal pushers, fine. Otherwise, let's be on our way. Our mission is to find the right bikes."

A few blocks away, we entered another bicycle shop. This one looked like a bike shop—oiled wood floors, parts hanging from the walls, upturned bike frames in various stages of repair and a greasy-handed proprietor who came out of the back room whistling "Daisy, daisy. . . ." He was obviously from that era.

By now, I had the confidence that comes with complete knowledge of a field. "What have you got in ten speeds?" I said with John Wayne resonance. Of course, John would have said six-shooters, but the effect was the same.

The little man, stooped by years, showed me his wares, including some reconditioned bikes which carried a "my word guarantee." Still, he threw no light on the question: What bikes do we really need? So we looked on. Five or six stores later, we found ourselves on Brunswick Avenue in Trenton, a few blocks north of the famous landmark erected to George Washington in commemoration of his Christmas Night march, 1776.

Outside a corner store were two large signs proclaiming this BERNIE'S BICYCLE SHOP, AUTHORIZED SCHWINN DEALER. I could see a large lineup of racing bikes just inside the door and hesitated going in. It was a Schwinn that Kermit the Creep rode, and for a second I saw myself dressed like Kermit in a leather football helmet, bent over a la Eddie Arcaro on Whirlaway. But Shirley walked ahead and before I knew it we were inside.

"Be right with you," called a genuinely friendly voice from behind the counter. How he was going to be right with us would be interesting to know, considering he had a dozen other people in the store. But this man, Bernie Knapp, I was to learn, is no ordinary bicycle shop proprietor.

"Oliver, Mrs. Thomas' bike, please. That will be $4.50, Ma'am. We'll toss in the brake shoe free. Tell your son not to back up on them, they'll fall out every time. Thank you."

"Tom, take a look in the back and make out your own order, and give me a better price than last time," he kidded a salesman.

"Now, you wanted a new tire. Do you want it mounted? Oliver, give this gentleman a new tire on this rim."

"And you, Sir? Yes, a fine bike. How old is your boy . . . well that's a nineteen-inch frame . . . he'll need a twenty-one . . . when is his birthday . . . Friday . . .

Just a minute, I'll call my wife at the other store. . . .
Honey, have you got a Super-Duper? Okay. Mark it sold.
I'll pick it up tomorrow. We have one over at the other
place. I'll deliver it Thursday."

And so it went. Finally, Bernie came over and introduced himself to us. He is a big, affable man of Polish
descent, who knows the bike business like no one I have
ever met. A plaque on his wall, partially hidden by a
stack of wire baskets, attests to his acumen: it proclaims
him the third leading Schwinn salesman in the country
for selling I don't know how many thousands of new
bikes in one year. (This was my first insight into the size
of the bicycle industry.)

Inside ten minutes, he had our situation doped out
cold. "You need a twenty-three-inch frame, your wife and
daughter twenty-ones, that's all they come in, and your
son needs a nineteen-inch.

"I'd suggest Schwinn five speeds. They're rugged and
easy to maintain. You'll be able to keep them going on
the road yourself."

"Me?" I laughed, "I can't fix a leaky faucet."

"Well, you're gonna' learn to fix bikes, Mr. Bauer," he
said firmly. "I equip you with all the tools and spare
parts you'll need—gear and brake cables, tire patch kit,
everything. If you have trouble, try to fix the bike yourself, 'cause if you get out on the road there ain't gonna'
be anyone to help you on a Saturday afternoon. Then, if
you can't fix it yourself (here's the handbook, read it
over a coupla' times), bring the bike back and *we* will
tackle the problem together. There are a few 'idiocies'

about 'em, but you can learn 'em." (I thought Bernie meant "idiosyncrasies," but later I learned that he was right: "idiocies" they were.)

Half an hour later, we loaded two new Schwinns into the back of the station wagon. (We had to order Laraine's and Steve's.) Bernie was still talking as we went out the door. "Don't overdo or you won't be able to get out of bed. Remember, build up gradually."

I smiled back at the advice. He didn't know that he was talking to a former third string center for the Montpelier (Ohio) High School Locomotive football team. I had gone through rugged conditioning regimens before. This would be nothing for that old center, Sizzle Snap Bauer.

4 Pass the Ben-Gay

"The name of the game is getting up the hills," some bicycle-philosopher out of the past once said, and I soon learned that, as Dizzy Dean would say, "He wasn't just awoofing, Partner."

The first hill of any consequence that we attempted was nearly my last. "Oxygen," I called out after pedaling twenty-five yards up the three-quarter-mile long Harrison Street grade in Princeton. There was no answer. When I gained enough strength to turn my head and look behind, I saw Shirley a few yards back with her tongue dangling like mine. Steve and Laraine had managed to ride a little farther than their parents, but not without considerable exertion.

"Let's ride, Daddy," said Christopher, who quickly took to our morning bicycle sorties like a bear to honey. That is, as long as we kept moving. Any delay and he became impatient.

After a couple of minutes of deep breathing, I climbed back aboard and again struggled violently with this obstacle of nature. Though it is recommended that one stay seated while trying to pedal uphill, I discovered there is leverage to be gained by standing and applying full weight to the task. This I did, but without any improvement in distance covered or pain relieved.

In the next twenty-five yards, my bike snaked imperceptibly ahead, while I was swinging and swaying over the crossbar in a sideways motion not foreign to fanciers of the Oriental belly dance. Finally, I dropped off and grabbed the machine to keep it and Chris from rolling backwards. The last thing I wanted to do was cover ground I had already captured!

Now, in addition to being winded, my head was spinning, my stomach aching and my thighs and calves complaining as if the devil in the Ben-Gay commercials had selected me for his rusty chains.

By the time Shirley reached me, I had a suggestion: we should walk our animals to the top. She tried to answer, but was still gasping; yet she was able to nod her head in approval and soon we began hoofing it. Ten minutes later, we reached the pinnacle and climbed back on the bikes again. Exhilaratingly, we raced downhill, streaking for home. Unfortunately, the free trip ran out short of Jefferson Road and we had two more battles before we reached our front door. Once there, we found our two older siblings lying prostrate on the porch, immobile.

After unbuckling Chris and lifting him out of his jump-seat, I staggered inside and collapsed into the first chair. Shirley, who had beaten me, looked like a stretcher case draped over the sofa, both hands cradling her head.

"You shouldn't sit down immediately after strenuous exercise," I said, quoting from page 104 of the *Track and Fieldman's Training Handbook*. "Runners should always walk awhile after a race."

"Fine. Walk around the block twice, once for me," she answered.

In a few minutes, bodies began to show life. Exhaustion slowly transformed into fatigue and fatigue into thirst and thirst into hunger. One by one we wandered into the kitchen for breakfast, and after a hearty meal, set about our regular duties.

For the first few days, night couldn't come soon enough. We were all bushed. In fact the children went off to bed after finishing homework without any encouragement, a novelty, believe me. TV stood silent for the first time in memory, and even the eleven o'clock news was found to be dispensable. By nine or nine thirty, Mama and Papa, night owls of long standing, were roosting with the chickens.

Following Bernie Knapp's advice, we tried to work into

shape gradually, but we weren't sure for a while whether we were building up or tearing down. We all took turns massaging one another's backs and legs. After the Harrison Street hill, we attacked the Washington Road gutbuster. This one, which runs through the University, was tabbed Mt. Misery by the kids and, like Harrison Street, we took many a walk up it.

In the beginning, for the first couple of weeks, we stayed close to home, limiting our pre-breakfast treks to two or three miles. Then, gathering all our strength, we ventured out toward Educational Testing Service, toward Carnegie Lake and Kingston and Penn's Neck. Yet, each increase in distance brought new cries from our muscles. I told the rest of the troupe that pain is the price which must be paid by anyone serious about getting into condition. Mutinously, they argued that the cost was exorbitant.

As part of my psychological warfare, I began gathering materials on cycling. From newspapers and magazines, I clipped articles. I sent for books, joined organizations, subscribed to cycling publications, and information poured in. The bulk of it was from such cycling boosters as the League of American Wheelmen, *Bicycling* magazine, the International Bicycle Touring Society, the Bicycle Institute of America (promoters of bike routes all over the country), the Schwinn people and American Youth Hostels.

From these sources, I gleaned helpful tips and encouraging information which I passed on to the rest of the clan. For example, from one handbook, we found advice on the proper use of gears on the hills. Often, in our early workouts, we would pedal furiously down a hill and continue "racing our motors" up the next climb for as far as we could maintain the pace. We wouldn't attempt to change gears until we had lost most of our momentum, then with wild motion we would try to get into an easier gear before the bike coasted to a stop. More often than not, we lost the fight.

The secret, we learned, was to ride down a hill in, say, fifth gear, the hardest pedaling, usually coasting the last part of the descent. This allows the rider a chance to recoup his breath in preparation for the next climb. When the hill flattens out, one should begin pedaling again. If the hill isn't too steep, speed can be maintained a good way into the climb. However, at the point where pedaling becomes difficult and the bike begins to lose velocity, one should shift down into a middle gear. A properly working bike will shift in two or three revolutions of the pedals. Finally, if the hill hasn't been topped, one should shift into first, the easiest and lowest gear. The key is timing. Before the bike's speed peters out the shift must be made.

One uplifting reprint from *Bicycling* magazine reached us at an opportune time. The article by a Mr. J. E. Grambart of Atlantic City, New Jersey, described a two-week, 565-mile tour he took with a cycling group through the mountains of Vermont and New Hampshire. At the time, we were struggling with the comparatively level terrain of New Jersey, and could not conceive of anyone attempting to tangle with the mountains of the Northeast.

But Mr. Grambart gave us hope. Early in the trip, he noted, "I found it expedient to top the steepest hills on foot. I'd manage to pump myself nearly to the top, shifting frantically (and rather clumsily) down through the gears as I lost momentum, only to find that my feet were the ultimate gear after all. This was a common experience for many of us during the first week. But by the end of the first week some of us began to find the planned fifty-to-seventy-mile daily rides too short . . . I rediscovered the legs and lungs of my early youth and the hills really flattened out."

The *coup de grâce* was to learn that Mr. G was in his fifties!

I also learned a little history about the bicycle and the growth of its popularity. For example, I was surprised to read that the bicycle only recently passed its sesquicentennial, having come into being in 1816 at the hand of a German named Baron Karl Drais von Sauerbronn. Calling it a *draisine* (or hobby horse), the Baron equipped his invention with most everything but pedals. It reportedly rode well enough down hill, but was a real drag returning. Back to the drawing board.

In 1840, pedals were brazed onto the vehicle in the Scottish blacksmith shop of Kirkpatrick MacMillan, who was no doubt thought to be the victim of a hoof in the head when villagers first saw him ride around the town square on his two wheeler. It is a fact that he got into a heated *imbroglio* with local fuzz over his excessive speed, resulting in an arrest and fine.

The bike, a wooden-wheeled model called a boneshaker, was introduced to America in 1866; however, it received a less than enthusiastic reception. Too expensive and rough riding was the public's general verdict. Within two years, however, American models were to be fitted with hard rubber tires and wire spokes, and interest in the bicycle began to build.

By the 1890's, bicycling was growing by leaps and bumps. Riders found that speed could be increased if they enlarged the size of the front wheel and decreased the size of the rear, which resulted in the ordinary bike, featuring a 64-inch front wheel and a 12-inch wheel behind. Though this model would travel a blazing twenty miles an hour, riders had trouble keeping their balance, and more often than not found themselves on the ground before completing a short spin around the block.

Inflatable rubber tires were the innovation which put bicycling on the transportation map—pneumatic tires and a more reasonable price tag. Though most bikes were one hundred dollars or more in the 1890's, the cost was considerably less than the ordinary, for example: it was over three hundred dollars. With a better ride available, the bike craze was on. Clubs were formed, and touring became popular, as did racing.

In 1899, a man named Charles M. Murphy, as a result of a boast or bet (or both), challenged a Long Island Railroad train, claiming he could keep up with it for a mile. On a special board track, Murphy pedaled one mile in 57.8 seconds and thereby gained for himself international fame as Mile-A-Minute Murphy. That same year, Marshall Walter Taylor, known as Major Taylor, won the world championship and was recognized as the fastest cyclist of all time. When he won the U.S. title a year later, he became one of the first American Negroes to so distinguish himself in any sport.

Shortly after the turn of the century, my research revealed, cycling suffered a severe setback and looked to be a passing fad. The automobile was the head turner. Among the deserters was Henry Ford, who was in the bike business at that time.

Though six-day bike racing developed into a strong spectator-drawing sport in the years immediately following with its stars pulling down salaries of $15,000 a year, recreational cycling dwindled. Even the six-day riders pumped off the scene during the depression years, and by 1940 most Americans considered cycling a pastime for youngsters.

It was different in Europe, of course. There, cycling continued to provide economical transportation and healthy recreation. After World War II, such events as the Tour de France, a twenty-two-day, 2,700-mile race, became more popular than ever, attracting the fastest pedalers from all over the world to compete for fame and fortune. The winner of France's big event reportedly can earn $100,000 in the year of his victory.

Adult interest in cycling did not revive in America until the early 1960's. Then, suddenly, there came the physical fitness craze. People had more time and money and cycling rocketed back into prominence.

A pamphlet from the Bicycle Institute of America explained the origin of *Bikeways* signs I had been seeing all over the country. Bikeways, I learned, had their birth in 1962 in Homestead, Florida, as a result of Mr. and Mrs. George Fichter's desire for marked safety routes to remind motorists that they were sharing the road with cyclists. The Fichters' idea caught on, and today there are hundreds of Bikeways throughout the country with many more on the way. Former Secretary of Interior Stewart Udall has recommended that at least 200,000 miles of roadways be specially marked for cycling, within the next decade.

But the most significant evidence of renewed interest in cycling is in the number of Americans riding bikes today. As a result of a more than 100 percent increase in new bike sales in the last ten years, cycling is now the number one participation sport in America with an estimated 60,000,000 pedalers.

When I shared all this information with my novices, they were duly impressed.

By the beginning of our third week, we had worked up to trips of between five and eight miles before breakfast. To the seasoned cyclist, especially those who race, this sounds like a warm-up I know, but let me assure you that for our family of five, it was plenty. If we responded alertly to the six o'clock alarm, there was often time enough to circle the lake or ride out U.S. 1, along the wide, paved berm to Clarksville, and then back in on Quakerbridge Road, a ten-mile round trip.

The first time we made the Clarksville run was on a Saturday, and we interrupted the ride for breakfast at

one of those great U.S. 1 diners the wise truckers frequent. The trip out was pure joy as a little breeze nudged
us along. However, coming back that day we came to
grips with a new adversary: a head wind. It hit us straight
on and brought moans and groans from all. Yet, we made
it, limp and gasping.

Another foe those early April mornings was cold and
rain. Though the troops petitioned me to call off a number of rides because of inclement weather, I insisted that
athletes train every day and we did, with few exceptions.
Clad in windbreakers, scarfs, gloves, stocking caps and
other winter garb, we fought the elements with Admiral
Byrd resolve, often returning chilled through. The stand-
ard joke on those forty-five-degree mornings was that we
should ride to Washington's Crossing on the Delaware
River for our vacation. The park which marks General
George's boat ride is about twenty miles from Princeton!

By the end of April, we had worked our way up to
fifteen-mile rides, and we were now ready for an all-
morning test. On April 27, a Saturday, we set out for
Hopewell, ten miles away, "in the rain at 7:30," the daily
log I kept informs me. Donning some newly purchased
bright orange rain gear (dubbed Kermit-wear), we were
pleased to find that it was both warm and waterproof.
Furthermore, there was little likelihood of any motorist
not seeing us, a fact that disturbed Laraine greatly.

"We look ridiculous in these," complained our thirteen-
year-old fashion consultant. Even so, she slithered into
the pants, zipped up her jacket and tied the hood under
her chin.

Shirley's problem in the rain was her glasses. If they weren't splotched with water to the point that she couldn't see, they were fogged over. However, there was no question of her taking them off—and staying on the road.

The only real shortcoming we found at this time with the rain gear was in the material's strength. On my second leg-swing over the crossbar, there was a resounding rip and my trousers smiled from one knee to the other. Even with this customized air conditioning, I stayed dry, however, and by the time we reached Hopewell, the sky had cleared and the sun was out.

Though we had eaten lightly before leaving home, our appetites had returned by the time we pulled into Hopewell, so we headed for the town bakery where we bought a large supply of their sweetest rolls. Adding coffee and milk, we were greatly refreshed.

We circled back to Princeton on secondary roads, north and east, and as noon approached we hit Route 27 near Kingston and Carnegie Lake. At the lake we came upon a number of picnickers on hand to watch an afternoon of crew racing. We decided to join them and there, with the lake for a backdrop, we unpacked our lunch and ate. We had covered twenty-four miles in a little over four hours. Though tired, no one was complaining.

"Pretty good," I said. "Now if we can just put an afternoon together with a morning of that distance, and do it consistently, we can start thinking about our vacation trip. Do you believe you could ride another twenty-five miles this afternoon?"

"Sure," answered Steve, who was getting enthused.

"Laraine?"

"Well, maybe."

"Shirley?"

"Pass the mustard."

5 Is There a Mechanic in the House?

The day following our twenty-four-mile success, I announced that we were now ready for a two-day weekender, and suggested that we schedule it for the following Saturday and Sunday, May 4 and 5.

"Where would you like to ride?" I asked the kids. "We could go into Bucks County in Pennsylvania, or maybe you'd rather head for the shore."

"If we go to the shore, can we go swimming?" Steve wanted to know. His mother answered him with a look.

"Well, even if we can't swim," said Laraine, "I'd rather go east than toward Pennsylvania. Too many hills." All agreed that she had a good point, so it was decided. I studied the map and charted in my mind a trip toward Long Branch by way of Hightstown and Freehold. Then, I figured, we would go south along the beach to Asbury Park, and return to Princeton via Route 33. The round trip would run about eighty miles.

"We better get the tent out of the attic as well as the sleeping bags and some basic camping supplies," I suggested. Though I intended to stop at a motel our one night away, carrying camping equipment seemed a good precaution in case of mechanical difficulty. Furthermore, it was about time we started working with our weight handicaps, for if we did indeed make a long camping trip by bike, each of us would be required to tote an additional twenty-five or thirty pounds. Just how we were going to pull that much weight was one small detail I had not yet worked out. Christopher created an additional logistical problem, because with him riding with me, my capacity for extra gear would be limited to a front basket. Shirley, Laraine and Steve would therefore get the brunt of the load.

A more immediate concern was bicycle maintenance. Up until then, I had done little repair on our Schwinns because, being new, they needed little attention. But before making a trip to the ocean, I wanted to familiarize myself with the basic operation of the bike. Otherwise, we might be in for a long walk home. Bernie Knapp had suggested that I tear the bikes down and attempt to put them back together, but at the time I was doing the final writing and editing on a book, and had no time for such folly. Folly, I say, because with my mechanical aptitude, it was 10 to 1 that once the bikes were dismantled they would never be the same again.

I don't know where I was as a boy when other kids were taking watches apart, trying to figure out what made them tick. I guess I was out selling Cloverine salve, earning a new pocket watch of my own. (My poor grandmother: I'll bet she bought a gross of that white salve just to help me win premiums.)

Apprehensive as I was about putting a wrench on the bikes, there were a couple of genuine problems which had developed, so one night after dinner I went to the basement and carefully disassembled Laraine's front brake mechanism. The problem was quite simple: when she applied the front hand brake nothing happened. In an attempt to restore braking action in the caliper assembly (that's what the book called it), I followed each procedure to the letter. The manual explained that adjustment was a simple matter, and it was: something like putting together an eighty-four-pump toy gas station on Christmas Eve.

An adjusting barrel was the first point of attack. If that didn't cure the problem, the book said to tighten or loosen the brake cable. The object was to get the brake shoes on either side of the wheel to within an eighth of an inch of the rim. I did as instructed, but when I had finished one brake shoe was so in love with the wheel that it wouldn't move, while the other shoe was so wide it appeared to be signaling for a left turn.

As I wound up to throw the wrench, my most graceful move with tools, I heard someone coming down the steps. It was Shirley with a cup of tea. Such timing. She knew that I would soon need soothing and a cup of tea was her idea of a tranquilizing potion.

"This part is going to need replacing," I told her. She had heard that one before. Whenever our car develops trouble, I always lift the hood for effect, drop my head inside and fiddle with the oil stick. Then, I emerge with this report: "Serious. I'll have to call a mechanic."

Later that week in the back of Bernie's, the head man had the brake shoes adjusted thirty seconds after he began working on them. When he had completed the job, he undid his work and handed me the wrench. "Now you try." I did and to my surprise, succeeded.

It was the same story when I tried to repair Steve's *dérailleur*, the mechanism which moves the chain from one sprocket to another. He could not get his bike into first, the easiest pedaling gear, so once again I studied the manual, following each direction. After an hour's frustration, the chain not only refused to mesh in the first gear, but it would not seat in the fourth or fifth either. Back to Bernie. This time I put the watch to him to see how long it would take him to get the problem solved. In exactly one minute and forty seconds, the chain was running up and down the sprockets like a trained monkey.

Not so with Shirley's bike. Thinking I had learned something from watching the Old Master attend to Steve's bike, I was prepared for any malfunction, or so I thought. But Shirley's *dérailleur* did not respond to any of my ministrations and off to Trenton I drove again, bike in back of station wagon.

"You're late for work," Bernie called out when he saw me coming, intimating that I was there often enough to be on the payroll.

"Very funny, but let me see you fix this one in a minute, forty seconds," I challenged.

Bernie rolled up his sleeves and began the operation with practiced moves Dr. Ben Casey would have envied. Five minutes passed. Ten. He cussed a little. Fifteen minutes. He threw a screwdriver. He adjusted and re-adjusted, cleaned and oiled. Studied. Perspiration stood out on his forehead. Though I wore a concerned look on my face, inside I couldn't have been more happy. He couldn't fix it either!

Finally, at the twenty-two-minute mark, he threw a wrench and reached for a huge rubber mallet which hung on the wall. With careful aim, he smashed the mallet against the *dérailleur*. I was horror stricken. The book advised tender loving care for this part, especially. It is an intricately working, precision made mechanism—imported from Europe. And if that wasn't enough to win it respect, its seven dollar price tag was.

"Where in the Schwinn manual does it tell you to use a mallet?" I asked.

Holding the rubber cudgel skyward as in the baking

soda ad, Bernie turned sage: "When all other means fail, gentle but firm persuasion is the court of last resort." Then, he wiped his hands clean and with cool disdain cranked the pedals. Humbled, the chain fell into line without a smidgen of resistance.

On Friday evening of that week, we packed the camping gear into waterproof duffel bags, loaded it onto the bikes and strapped it down with elastic grippers. The following morning we were up at six and, after a big breakfast, rode off into the rising sun.

It was an idyllic spring day and the cycling went well except for a few minor problems. Outside Hightstown, ten miles away, Steve slipped off the pavement and ran his bike aground, into a mound alongside the road. The dirt dug into his *dérailleur* and when he pulled the bike away, the chain dragged on the pavement. I feared the worst, a broken part, but after cleaning out the grass and grit and retracking the chain, everything seemed to be in order, so we continued.

Though Route 33 was a more heavily traveled road than we would have preferred, we had little choice but to stick with it until we reached Freehold, twenty miles away. At Freehold, we headed northeast on 537, a lesser-used road lined with beautiful farms, many featuring workout tracks for harness horses. Freehold, as many will know, is the home of Freehold Raceway and it is a hotbed of harness racing enthusiasts. When we needed rest that day, we often stopped opposite a field of grazing mares and their still-nursing foals.

By one thirty, we had covered thirty miles and our stomachs were growling for food. When a truck stop came into view, we picked up the pace and hightailed it in for lunch. Though I think she's about right as is, Shirley had counted on losing a few pounds from cycling, but she began to doubt that it would be the case, judging from her enormous appetite.

After lunch we rode another five miles and then chose a park for Chris' afternoon nap. Unfortunately, there was a pond nearby and he spent most of the period running with his brother and sister while his mother and father catnapped under a tree. Though we were pooped, our muscles were not hurting as much as a couple of weeks before. It was a sign we were gaining.

By three thirty, we continued on our way, turning south and following the shoreline toward Asbury Park, but it was an abbreviated ride. First, I heard Chris make a little puppy whimper.

"What's the trouble, Buddy?" I inquired. There was no answer. Before I could turn around, I felt a thud in the middle of my back. As Chris had been running his matchbox cars up and down the hills of my spine, I thought I had no doubt been bumped by an Austin Healy. We were riding in traffic at the time, so I could not stop. Instead I put my left hand around behind my back to feel what he was up to. Just then, I got jolted again. What I touched was his head, dropping forward against my back. He was asleep!

At the next corner, we turned out toward the beach and came to a stop on a stretch of public sand. There with Shirley's help I unstrapped the boy and placed him on the ground with his security blanket, an item we never cycled without. For nearly an hour, he snoozed while Laraine and Steve waded in the icy surf.

About five o'clock, we rode into Asbury Park and found a motel on the west edge of town. After dinner, I checked my cyclometer. We had covered fifty-one miles.

The next morning we took to the road at eight A.M., and with the exception of a time-out for breakfast and a Coke break, we rode straight back to Princeton, covering thirty-five miles by one o'clock.

As we neared Princeton, I turned around and called to Shirley. "We're almost there."

"I know," she shouted back.

"Oh, I wasn't sure you could see that well." The day before while unloading the bikes, one of the elastic grippers with steel hooks on the end had popped up and hit her glasses. One lens was shattered, but fortunately no glass got into her eye. Still, she didn't have a spare pair of glasses along so she had to wrap adhesive tape around the broken lens and make do. I told her passersby would think one of two things: either cycling is a terribly rough sport or she was working for the Hathaway shirt people!

6 "Mission Impossible"

Our round trip of eighty-six miles on May 4 and 5 proved to us beyond any doubt that we could make an extended trip by bike, so the next order of business was to select a destination. I held to my original suggestion: coast to coast. Shirley doubted that we could maneuver the mountains of Pennsylvania, not to mention the rough terrain and desert of the Southwest. She was for a less auspicious undertaking: Florida, where her parents and grandparents live. The difference between New York to Deland, Florida, and New York to Los Angeles is 1,100

versus 3,000 miles. Laraine and Steve leaned toward the
west because we had just made the trip south for two
weeks over Christmas. So, Shirley capitulated and we
began working on the specific details.

Knowing the who (the five of us), the where (to California) and the how (by bicycle), we were left to resolve
the what (we needed to take), the when (we were going) and the why (a tenable reason to give our friends
and relatives).

The when was determined first by the kids' availability.
School was not scheduled to finish until the middle of
June, a little later than we wanted to get underway.
However, investigation showed that the last week was not
a full week, so with early tests they would be free after
the first week of June. As a writer, I have some flexibility
in schedule and I began to isolate the months of June
and July for our trip. By hustling, I figured I could finish
up my current obligations by the first of June to coincide
with the children's vacation.

Of course, school would not begin until September, but
I had several fall writing commitments and knew that I
would need to be back by the middle of August, giving
us ten weeks at most. Dividing ten weeks into 3,000
miles figured 300 miles a week, so if we could average
50 miles a day—a reasonable goal we were told by more
experienced cyclists—we would have time to spare.

The "why" of our trip might seem obvious; in fact I
am sure it was to our children: we were doing it for the
adventure. But face it, adults are more complicated
creatures. I needed a more serious excuse. The best I

could do at that time was to say, "I'm going to research
a book." True enough, I had been gathering material for
a camping book and, because we were going to camp
as well as cycle, it added up. Still, the bona fide purpose
for which I was looking didn't come to the surface until
a week or two before our departure.

One evening at dinner, Laraine quite casually mentioned a discussion her eighth grade class had had that
day in social studies. The debate, a lofty one for eighth-
graders I felt, centered around America's position in the
world, and the direction our country is heading. When I
asked Laraine the class's conclusion, she said it was
"mixed, confused." I was pleased to know they understood the situation!

"On one hand," she began, "we say we are helping
Vietnam by protecting her from Communism, but other
countries—even some of our friends—say we are murder-
ers, bombing women and children. Pass the potatoes,
please." There was a shuffle of dishes and then she continued:

"We also talked about Martin Luther King's death.
On one hand, we think democracy is wonderful and that
everyone should have freedom. We are all for inde-
pendence for new countries, but when it comes down to
our own Negroes, we don't give them the same things
we have. Isn't that right?" The question was for me.

"Yes, we have some problems, but—." I started to ped-
dle my brand of propaganda, then stopped. "But what
do you think our direction as a country is?" She shook
her head.

"Do you think most Americans are bigots?"

"Bigots?" she questioned.

"Mean, full of hate, unfair to minorities—Negroes, Puerto Ricans, Jews." She didn't know. Again, I had to restrain myself from giving an adult's version. Instead, I had another approach.

"This summer we are going to see America up close. I want both you and Steve to observe people's nature. And when we get home, we'll talk about our country some more. I think you'll both have some things to say, if you keep your eyes and ears open."

With that the conversation ended, but now we had our "why" for making the trip. I was intrigued myself with the idea of taking another hard look at America, for in recent days my eyes, too, had been reporting strange findings that made me anxious not only about our country's general state of health, but about the placeboes being prescribed by many of her doctors.

I had traveled back and forth across the length and breadth of this land by car and train and plane, usually at from sixty to six hundred miles an hour, but now I was going to see her at a much more leisurely pace, say at eight or ten miles an hour. It sounded like the ideal way to discover the real America.

Day by day, other pieces of the puzzle fell into place. After inquiring from a number of cycling organizations, asking for advice on routes, I sat down with maps and began marking out our itinerary. "Travel the back roads, the secondary routes," was the counsel from all corners.

Sometimes this seemed easier to do than others. In Pennsylvania for example, through the mountain range, there weren't that many choices. Of course, turnpikes and interstate highways do not permit cycling, so that narrowed the options. From topographical maps, we saw that Pennsylvania was going to be our first big test.

"If we can get through the mountains there," Shirley said, "we should have fairly easy going until the Southwest."

Meanwhile, we continued our daily conditioning routine and I persevered in the maintenance department until I had more mechanical dexterity than I ever would have imagined.

We made two other overnight trips before D Day. One was into Pennsylvania, along the Delaware north to Frenchtown, east to Flemington, south to Pennington and back to Princeton, a round trip of sixty-five miles. It was a wild one.

First, we ran into some glass and two tires went flat almost simultaneously. Before I could get them patched and back on the bikes (we carried a patch kit and a small pump just like Model T days), it began raining, and before we could get into our gear we were soaked. Riding through a real downpour, we made our way to Frenchtown, hoping to stay there for the night; but the village had no motel, so we set out at five thirty for Flemington, eleven miles away. It was a hairy ride. The heavy rain cascaded down, driven into our faces by a stiff wind. And the traffic was heavier than any we had ever battled.

By six thirty, we had only covered about four miles and darkness was coming on fast. I began looking for a barn or garage that might be adequate to spend the night in, but found nothing. We had the tent along, but as we were cold and soaked already that was Option 27. Then, up ahead, I spotted a filling station with a pickup truck out front. Riding in advance of the others, I went inside and asked if we could hire the truck for a lift into town.

The proprietor said he was by himself, but another young man in the shop volunteered to drive the pickup if it was all right with the owner. He agreed and as soon as the rest of my wet pack arrived we loaded the bikes onto the truck and set out for town. Steve and I, riding in the back with the bikes, turned blue from the wind before we got there.

Inside the cab, Shirley, Chris and Laraine were hearing a fascinating story from the driver. Upon learning that we intended to go cross-country on the bikes, he revealed that he had ridden a horse from New Jersey to Chicago the summer before.

"Had to quit because the horse went lame," he said. "I'd like to try again, but I had my problems. In one town, they threatened to fine me for littering, though I suggested it was the horse which should be fined. And at several bridges, I was refused entry, so I went down below and forded the rivers on horseback."

At the motel, we changed into the clothes that had

remained dry in our duffel bags, and after warming up, journeyed across the street for a steak dinner. By the time we had finished, Chris was asleep and I had to carry him back to the motel.

The other conditioning excursion was a shakedown camping trip outside of Princeton. We made this one over Memorial Day, a little more than a week before our target date for leaving, June 7. Like the trip before, it rained during the night, but this time we managed to keep everything dry. Another milestone.

The last unanswered question, the "what" (we were going to take), was the toughest. Shirley was in charge of the wardrobe and she wisely selected as much wash and wear clothing as possible. It was apparent that we would need a laundromat every three or four days.

I decided that our sleeping bags were too bulky, so searched the market for lighter, more compact gear. An inquiry of the Coleman people in Wichita brought an offer from them to supply us with any sleeping bag in their line as well as any of their products we could use—tents, lanterns and stoves; but in the end, I chose four down bags manufactured by Black's of Ogdensburg, New York, and one Coleman bag. As for a stove, I tested the Coleman Sportsman, a great little three-pound, one-burner unit; a Swedish-made Optimus, one-and-a-half pounds; and a collapsible Sterno stove. I settled on the largest and the smallest—the Coleman and Sterno stoves.

As for a tent, we decided to stay with the bright

orange, German-made tent we had purchased in Freiburg the summer before. With a zippered front flap and sewed-in canvas floor, it would sleep the five of us cozily. Also, it was fast drying and, best of all, weighed only sixteen pounds, complete.

Shoes, hats, sun glasses, suntan lotion, first aid kit, eating and cooking utensils, dehydrated foods, toys and books for Christopher, flashlight, a compass . . . the list was endless. But by the first of June we were making progress.

One of the last things we did was to tell parents and grandparents of our plans. We figured it would be best to limit their pre-trip neurosis by keeping the news to the very end. When at last Shirley wrote them, phone calls followed from the appropriate directions.

"What about the traffic? Isn't it dangerous?"

"We're going to take secondary roads."

"What about protection? Is Fred going to take a gun?"

"No, Fred remembers his Army days and is afraid he'd shoot himself."

"Well, it all sounds like 'Mission Impossible' to us!"

As with any trip, preparation is endless and ours continued right up till the morning we left. For example, in our final week of rehearsal, a luncheon in New York reminded me that we had not yet arranged for the care of Heidi, our German Schnauzer. The way it came to mind was strange. I was dining in a little midtown restaurant with two friends when suddenly I spotted a familiar face sitting in one corner of the room. The man was a large-boned, outdoorsy-looking sort with a shock of gray-black, unruly hair and grizzly beard.

"Who's that?" I asked one of my dining companions, pointing the man out by description.

"Blackbeard," he answered.

"Peter Ustinov," guessed the other.

"No . . . no, it's John Steinbeck," I told them. And it was.

So, thanks to Mr. Steinbeck I remembered our dog Charley, ah, Heidi.

7 Forward Pedal

Friday morning, June 7—our getaway day—dawned sunny bright, but we didn't. Having been up until midnight the night before, we stumbled out of bed at five and began checking and rechecking our lists, trying to tie all loose ends. Leaving a house for ten weeks presents some additional complications over a regular two-week vacation, we discovered.

At six o'clock, Marge Ruszczyk, a friend from Bernie's Bicycle Shop, arrived with the panel truck. Marge had become very interested in our trip and had volunteered to transport our bikes the fifty miles to New York City's

Battery Park from where we would begin. It was our plan to take the ferry to Staten Island, then cycle across the island to the Outer Bridge Crossing, and there let Marge transport us into New Jersey. The reason we needed Marge again was because non-motorized traffic was prohibited on the bridge. In fact, there was no way to cycle off the island, we learned.

Shortly after Marge arrived, our good friends, Bob and Ann Westover came by, ready to chauffeur us to the city. Finally, it was time to lock up, after which we delivered our house keys and dog to the Hammonds next door—and we were off.

"Well, what have we forgotten?" I asked Shirley as we made the Harrison Street turn onto Route 1, and headed north toward New York.

"Our good senses," she answered with a laugh.

That we could have forgotten anything important was unlikely, judging from the loads we had on the bikes. As with any trip, we packed more than intended, but even so there was sure to be a missing can opener, matches, salt or handkerchiefs. It never failed. Any oversight would be a little more understandable this time, however, for it was a week all America had turned hazy-minded—the week Robert F. Kennedy's life was taken. For a short time, we considered postponing the trip, but any delay in schedule would have brought with it so many complications that we might have had to scrap the venture entirely. We decided it was now or never.

When news came that the Senator's body would lie in state that Friday at St. Patrick's Cathedral, I pondered taking the children to view the bier, but bumper-to-bumper traffic as we neared the city and radio reports describing the throng which had turned out in his honor made me reconsider.

The Westovers deposited us at the Battery, and went their way, leaving us to wait for the ten o'clock ferry. Photographers were scheduled to take some pictures of us then, so while we dallied I read the *Times*.

It was a one-story paper, though that one story was written from hundreds of angles. Laraine, as deeply moved as most people were by the tragedy, sat beside me, reading intently over my shoulder, and as she did our conversation about the condition of America came to mind.

One article pointed to a guilt we all felt, a corporate guilt that said we live in a country whose sickness had reached epidemic proportions. However, a statement by President Johnson rebutted the charge: "200 million Americans did not strike down Robert Kennedy." It was a poignant observation, and I called it to Laraine's attention.

Then, I asked her if she remembered what Anne Frank had written about the goodness of people? We had visited the Franks' attic refuge in Amsterdam the summer before and had seen a photostat of that statement pasted on the wall.

While Laraine puzzled over it, I clued her: "In spite of everything . . ."

". . . I think that people are really good at heart," she finished it.

After pictures had been taken, we made our way to the ferry and waited in line to board. While there, people leaned out of their cars and began talking with us. It was a rather strange occurrence. I am not one who considers New York an unfriendly city, but there is a kind of mind-your-own-business attitude which limits dialogue to utilitarian conversation. Still, it was apparent that we had stimulated people's inquisitive side, for they could not restrain themselves from questioning us at length. The only comparable conviviality that I could recall was the night Fun City's lights went out, and I was stranded in town, but that camaraderie was rooted in common inconvenience, and maybe fear. This was different.

Of course, there is truth in the old line that nothing primes conversation like dogs and kids, unless it's the weather, and our three younguns on bikes loaded with camping equipment proved to be consistent crowbars on silence. More often than not it was Christopher who served as catalyst.

"You've got the best seat, don't you, fellow," they would begin. Chris' response was normally a big smile which, like a tail-wagging dog, prompted more comments and eventually involved Mommy and Daddy.

It was Chris who magnetized a busload of Girl Scouts at the ferry. From North Carolina, the girls were on a two-week camping trip and more than casually interested in anyone harnessed with outdoor gear. Had we had some extra bikes, I think our party would have enlarged.

On the ferry, we rode our bikes to the bow of the ship for a good view of Miss Liberty, which we passed in the harbor on our way to Staten Island. During the twenty minute crossing, more people came to us and chatted. One young man, maybe twenty, though I would judge less, took out pad and pencil and began conducting an interview. He claimed he was with CBS-TV, though it took only a couple of questions to convince me that he was putting us on. Still I played along, willingly answering the questions he didn't want to ask for himself. When we docked, he said that he would call the story right in and that "no doubt, our cameramen will catch up with you later in the day." To no one's surprise, they didn't.

It was eleven o'clock by the time we pedaled off the ferry out onto the busy streets of Staten Island, and for the next two hours, we wove our way through the borough of Richmond. The day had turned into a blisterer with the temperature climbing into the high nineties, and by the time we pulled off for lunch, we were all dripping wet. After eating, we struggled on, reaching the Outer Bridge Crossing, fifteen miles from the ferry, about three o'clock. All of us, that is, except Shirley. She was lagging badly. About ten minutes later, she crept in, her face as red as a fire hydrant.

"It must be the weight we've got on," she said after she had caught her breath. "My bike just won't move." I was concerned about our poundage. It was more than anticipated, but I had no idea what we could jettison.

"I'll check your bike later," I told her. Right then, we had to find Marge and pack all of the bicycles back into the truck for portage across the bridge.

Once across the Hudson, we unloaded and bade Marge farewell. Watching her pull away left a lump in my throat; she was our last touch with home. We were now on our own.

The first order of business upon arriving in New Jersey was to find a rest spot for Chris. He was fussy and needed a nap. At a park near Metuchen, we all rested for better than an hour before continuing down Route 27, at rush hour, toward New Brunswick—where we hoped to spend the night. But near Edison we ran out of steam and began scouting for a motel. We had decided previously that we would camp some nights, motel others, and it was unanimous that we find beds that night.

Crossing over to Route 1 we located a place with pool, a requisite, and ten minutes later we were soaking our weary muscles. Chances are we would have stayed for hours, but we were also famished. So after the swim, we went across the way and gorged ourselves at a nearby diner, well frequented by truckers. I don't know whether we ate like truckers or threshers but we put away an unbelievable meal.

By nine we were in bed, drifting toward sleep when Steve's voice rose out of the darkness.

"How many miles did we get?"

"About thirty," I told him, rolling over.

"Isssh," he answered. "How many days will it take us at that rate?"

"Three hundred and sixty-five," said Laraine.

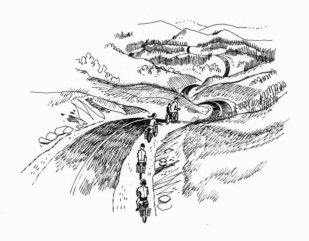

8 How Many Hills to Hillsboro?

Our second day out was no easier than the first, especially for Shirley. We rode from the motel to Highland Park, across the Raritan River into New Brunswick (where we took breakfast of juice, cereal, rolls and beverage on the move) and past the Rutgers campus on our way to Route 514—a beautiful back way across New Jersey through the pleasant communities of Middlebush, Millstone and Hillsboro Township. The name Hillsboro became a catch phrase early in our cycling experience. When someone at the rear of the pack would call ahead, se## How Many Hills to Hillsboro?

"How many miles to ———," whatever the next destination, the next in line would pass it on: "He wants to know how many hills to Hillsboro." Surprisingly, we passed through or near several Hillsboros on our excursion.

The first one was Hillsboro Township and the Hillsboro Shopping Center on Route 206 where Route 514 crosses. It lies just twelve miles north of Princeton, and was the site of an important early decision: what essentials were less essential than other essentials? The discovery that a brake shoe was dragging against the rear wheel of Shirley's bike alleviated some of her difficulty, but she was still laboring and I knew the only remedy would be to lighten her load. Laraine and Steve were also huffing and puffing under their handicaps, though to a lesser degree.

Finding a large shade tree near the shopping center, we unstrapped our bags and sorted through our gear, item by item. Food was the first thing to go. We would have to limit our rations to needs for the next meal and little else. The one-burner gas stove, which weighed four pounds with cover, was next to go into the dispensable pile. We would cook over Sterno.

Then, we turned our attention to the one oversized sleeping bag. If we disposed of it, we would have to figure another sleeping arrangement for Chris. Shirley concluded that he could wear heavier sleepers every night and sleep in one of the sheet sleeping sacks we carried for hosteling. Of course, he had his security blanket, so we decided to jettison one bag. Gain: five pounds.

A polyethylene bag containing rubber footwear which was more bulky than weighty was next. I was happy to part company with this package because I had thought it unnecessary from the start. Shirley, in defense of dry feet, had persisted. Now, if we got drenched we would have to find relief in an extra pair of socks or the second pair of shoes we each carried.

There were a few other odds and ends (including our movie camera) that we left in Hillsboro for later pickup, making the total weight reduction about twenty-five pounds. It was to prove a wise move in the weeks ahead. One other adjustment was a reassignment of the tent (but not stakes and poles) to my front basket, a ten-pound addition for me.

When we left Hillsboro after a pickup lunch, we were not only lighter physically, but psychologically, and we made good time the rest of the afternoon, reaching Route 202 about four o'clock. Shortly after turning onto this more traveled highway, Chris' head banged me in the back, a now-recognized signal, and we pulled over to rest, about eight miles from our day's destination which was Lambertville on the Delaware River. Though the heat was intense, and our noses were reddened despite liberal applications of Coppertone, we were holding up better than the afternoon before.

It was nearly five o'clock when we rode on, battling some hilly terrain as we neared Mount Airy, just three miles away from our stop. There, with appetites already pleading, we ran into an irresistible invitation, what at first seemed an aromatic mirage. Across Route 202, riding on a stream of smoke, was the most fragrant smell a hungry cyclist could imagine. We rode just a block off the road and found its source: an annual fireman's barbecue. Over huge outdoor pits were hung hundreds of chickens on bedspring-looking grills. The operation reminded me of my pizza-baking days. After college, Shirley and I had launched a pizza restaurant in Ohio as a way to support my writing career. It was successful enough that within a year we owned two restaurants and were wholesaling to a third. One of our come-ons was a huge exhaust fan which sent whiffs of pepperoni, oregano and mozzarella cheese out into the street, casting a Sicilian spell over passersby. I remember one guy telling me that when he stepped out of the theater down the street, his nose said goodby to hot buttered popcorn and hello to Bauer's Pizza.

We rode into the fireman's ball, pulled up a chair and ate chicken until we couldn't eat any more. What a hospitable group of people! When we inquired about a place to camp that night, preferably on the Delaware where we thought we could take a swim, several invitations were extended from residents who lived nearby.

"Here's my phone number."

"Here's my address."

"Give me a call, we'll pick you up in our truck." In the end, we thanked them all but camped on the river, just south of the bridge leading into New Hope, Pennsylvania. A few others had pitched tents nearby.

Though the Delaware has a mucky bottom and is less than crystal clear, we had a refreshing swim, and then turned in. At least the kids did. Shirley and I sat for a few minutes outside the tent watching the last glimmer of light fade behind the Pennsylvania hills across the river. A group of young people sat around a fire not far away, singing softly to the accompaniment of a guitar. As night deepened, the number of lights across the river increased. Some of them belonged to the restaurant near the Bucks County Playhouse, one of our favorite summer theater spots along with St. John Terrell's Music Circus, north of Lambertville. The two river towns make a charming community, one that has been adopted by a host of people in the arts.

Pointing in the direction of the Bucks County Playhouse, Shirley said: "Remember the night we saw Arthur Godfrey in *Our Town?*"

How could I forget. That performance prompted me to arrange an interview with him—a most memorable interview—but that's another story.

On June 9, Sunday, we walked our bikes across the fog shrouded Delaware Bridge into Pennsylvania.

"Our third state in as many days," the kids boasted. However, it was going to be our third state for a good many days to come. Mama Mia!

9 Up, Up, Up

In the last half dozen years, we have crossed Pennsylvania by car a couple of dozen times, driving back and forth between our home in New Jersey and our old homestead in northwest Ohio. The one-way trip takes about twelve hours, seven of which are spent traversing Pennsylvania—359 miles from the Delaware Memorial Bridge to the Ohio line. Never had we traveled through the state by any route other than the Pennsylvania Turnpike, though we'd considered it, wondering what it would be like off the speedway.

On bikes we got our chance to find out. Driven from the Turnpike and Interstate routes which prohibit non-motorized traffic, we took to the older, less journeyed roads with their bumpier surfaces, their snakiness and their steepness. And though we shadowed the Turnpike much of the way, traveling the same general area, we soon discovered why it took twice as long to drive the state thirty years ago. Where the Turnpike goes around mountains, cuts them down to kittenish hills or burrows beneath them, old highways like Route 30, which we chose much of the time, battle the heights head on.

The roads by today's standards are a safety council's nightmare—narrow and twisting. Yet, discounting the safety factor, these nearly forgotten routes, lined with ghost motels and restaurants and gas stations, offer some rare scenic treats of this blessed state, an outdoorsman's paradise. Then, too, beside magnificent vistas there are still a few Burma Shave rhymes.

Despite the state's bounteous natural beauty, we had difficulty appreciating her for a while. She was too torturous. Our common trepidation of the mountains proved to be well founded, for they almost smothered our trip in its infancy, and had it not been for the humiliation, we would have quit inside a few days I am sure. To the topographical experts, particularly the mountain-climbing breed, I know Pennsylvania is looked upon as a mere rolling plain; but to novice bicyclers like us, weighted down with all of life's necessities, she seemed nothing short of Blanc, Everest and the Matterhorn.

Our difficulties were myriad, but in the main they centered on these:

1. Though we had conditioned daily for better than two months, we had not put trips of fifty miles back to back for any sustained period, so we required a new type of conditioning.

2. We had trained in relatively flat New Jersey, whereas our first major test was a completely different terrain.

3. We had not trained long enough with full equipment.

4. Under heavier use, the bikes developed some problems that slowed and frustrated us. Just when it seemed we were about to have a good day, a flat, a broken gear cable or a *dérailleur* malfunction would brake our caravan to a halt.

5. We hit steaming temperatures straightaway, which required some special strategy. Too often, we rode late into the evening, quitting at dark— too late to eat and get bedded down in time for an early start the following day. The result was often a nine or nine thirty start, which soon had us riding in the worst heat of the day. Sooooo—we had some things to learn.

Checking my daily log, a laconic record of our movements, I can report the following in our early sparring rounds with Pennsylvania:

June 9, Sunday

> After some early morning fog, which required our
> lights, the day turned sunny and hot. We rode Route
> 202 (in rather heavy traffic at times) through Doyles-
> town and Montgomeryville, bypassing Norristown on
> our way to Route 23. Before we reached that high-
> way, however, we cycled through the village of Au-
> dubon, named after the famous painter of birds.

Audubon, the town, is worth a longer visit than we
made. Located just off Route 363, north of Valley Forge,
it features the first home in America of John James
Audubon. Built in 1762, the large stone house sits mag-
nificently above a small creek which rambles through the
134-acre property known as Mill Grove. Its story is another fascinating piece of American history.

Once owned by John Penn, a descendant of William,
it came into the hands of Frenchman Jean Audubon, the
wildlife painter's father, in 1789. The property was rich
in copper deposits and, in 1804, Audubon sent his nine-
teen-year-old son to oversee the place, but young Audubon
had other interests. During the two years he stayed at
Mill Grove, he reportedly was more captivated by its
abounding wildlife than its mineral wealth, and therefore
he spent most of his time observing and painting birds
and animals.

In the attic of the two-story house, Audubon set up a
studio (which has been recreated) for the purpose of
painting and taxidermy, and throughout the home are
hung reproductions of many of the paintings which made

him internationally famous. In addition to the thousands of visitors who come annually to tour the Audubon house, many individuals and groups come to roam Mill Grove and observe the wildlife in the same setting the renowned naturalist did when he first came here from France.

My interest in Audubon, the man, was aroused some years back while I was still in college. In need of two more hours of credit in science, I was nudged into an ornithology course by a friend who assured me that it would be a snap, a cakewalk, a sure "B."

So I enrolled only to discover that I had been badly mistouted. The first ill omen came when I learned that *Bird Watching 101* convened at 8:00 A.M.—an intolerable hour for my species, *Striges noctis* (night owl). But that was only the beginning. When I reached class the first day, I was handed two papers listing assignments for the term. One paper told of the required reading. It included such charismatic book titles as *Mating Habits of the Ibis, Waterfowl of the Okefenokee, Learning to Imitate Our Feathered Friends' Songs* and *How to Tickle a Purple Martin Pink*. The other paper was a schedule of field trips, all beginning at 5:00 A.M.

November 2	Grebe's Pond
November 11	Parker's State Park
	(with Ranger Wildcat Riley)
November 14	Grosbeak Sanctuary
November 27	Thomas' Wildlife Reserve, etc.

In panic, I tried to withdraw in favor of *Formaldehyde 301*, but the bluebird of happenstance passed over me and a dean who could do a perfect crow call sent me back to class. I was a trapped dodo.

For a few weeks, I nodded my way through lectures on the anatomy of birds, their identifying songs, their footprints, their wing shapes, their egg colors and their migration patterns. To stay awake, I played several little games, one of which was matching bird characteristics with members of the class. Professor T, for example, was definitely a snowy-type owl. He had the hair, the nose and the eyes for one, though I have never seen an owl wearing horn-rimmed glasses. Also, he was full of wisdom, able to draw anthropomorphic parallels between birds and humans at the drop of a tail feather.

In the class itself, we had a number of interesting birds, such as common loons, swans, boobies and peacocks. Among the girls, we had Alice the Cardinal, a long, lean Rita Hayworth redhead; Cynthia the Bluebird, a knock-out with eyes the color of the Mediterranean Sea; Jean the Lovebird, who sat in the back of the room, holding hands with Hank the Hawk, a member of the basketball team. It was a love match made in heaven: Jean wrote with her right wing, uh, hand, Hank with his left, so they could hold hands and take notes at the same time.

Other than Hank, the male birds I remember are Bill the Blue Jay, a cocky, swaggering student who had had ornithology in high school or had earned a Boy Scout merit badge in bird watching. Whichever, he and the professor engaged in several vitriolic debates. One had to do with the speed of ducks. The teacher, I believe, said that a Canada goose was faster than a blue-winged teal. Bill the Blue Jay challenged. Though I don't know how the donnybrook was resolved, I do remember that the discussion lasted long enough to wash out a scheduled test. Mike the Myna Bird was also clever at such delaying tactics. Whenever he wasn't ready for an exam, he would come in with some cock-and-bull story about a bird he had seen on the way to class.

"It was a gorgeous bird," he would begin, usually looking skyward and raising his hands in a mystical arc in front of his face. "It was orange under the wings with a darker breast. It's feet were webbed and its bill was long and narrow as a new pencil."

Professor T would scratch his head, ask some questions, leaf through a nearby reference book, and query the class—especially Bill the Blue Jay.

"Did you hear it sing?" he would often inquire.

Mike the Myna Bird, looking at his watch, would whistle bird-like as long as the situation demanded.

Usually, Professor T made a guess, though sometimes he would reserve judgment until the next class, wanting more time to consider it.

I shall never forget our first 5:00 A.M. trip into the bush. Armed with binoculars and a *Field Guide to Birds*, we followed our leader on a cross-country march—ducks off to the pond. At the back of the column skipped Jean the Lovebird and Hank the Hawk, at least for a few minutes. Right after we identified a yellow-bellied, purple-billed berry picker's footprint, Lovebird and Hawk disappeared, but no one was too concerned. After all, they had their own binoculars and bird guides. We didn't see anything of them until much later, when Al the Albatross went fighting his way into a heavy thorn bush to get a closer look at a wren's nest. Part way into the thicket, he stepped on either Lovebird or Hawk, who had found the nest first, and said they were waiting for the wren to return.

Before *Ornithology 101* was over, I, too, became an enthusiastic bird watcher. Though I never did come to enjoy it at 5:00 A.M., it has proved an enormously entertaining outdoor sport over the years. And, of course, my interest has been passed on to my children. On the bicycle trip, we were always on the alert for a new bird to add to our list, which numbered several dozen different kinds. Unfortunately, many of them were casualties along the roads, victims of speeding cars. In particular, we saw several vibrant-blue buntings which had apparently run dead heats with automobiles.

After the town of Audubon, we rode on to Phoenixville, arriving at six-thirty. We were ready to call it a day, but could find no motel nor camp site, so we took a gasoline station attendant's advice and cycled to a swimming club a short way from town. There we swam and camped in a secluded woods behind the pool. It was a fine spot, except for mosquitoes. Thank heavens we bought Army surplus netting for our tent.

We rode forty-three miles that day, bringing the total from New York to 108 miles.

June 10, Monday

Worst hills so far. Rode from Phoenixville to Morgan-
town where we turned south on Route 10, aiming for
Lancaster, but by five o'clock we were way short and
bushed. It was hilly, windy and rain was coming on.
Near Honeybrook we came upon a farm pond and
asked if we might stay there. The owners gave their
permission to camp and swim—which we did. Though
short on rations, we managed by heating onion soup
over Sterno and fixing peanut butter sandwiches and
Kool-Aid. We had fresh strawberries and cookies for
dessert. We got to bed at nine, just before rain.
Mileage: a poor 27. Total: 135 miles.

June 11, Tuesday

Rolled wet tent (which added to our weight). Breakfast, a hearty one, at restaurant in Honeybrook. Off
toward Lancaster at 8:30, cool and foggy. Route
change from 10 to 340 at Compass, then on through
White Horse, Intercourse, Bird in Hand. . . .

I might add that we didn't get to Fertility or Paradise
this trip, but then . . . we've been to those exotic Lancaster County communities before. We did stop in
Amish country that day for the purpose of cleaning our
chains and sprockets with gasoline, which always im-
proves *dérailleur* action. I was tempted to inquire at
another garage, a general repair shop which practiced
an interesting form of negative advertising, but decided
against it. Outside the shop's door was posted a sign
which read NO TOURISTS. Since this was Pennsylvania

Dutch country with a good many Amish families about, I took the sign to mean that only those in *that* religious persuasion need stop. ("He doesn't believe the Bible verse about entertaining angels unaware," said Shirley.)

Maybe the sign caught our attention, because it was so cold and excluding, whereas we had been the recipients of unrestrained, extroversive hospitality everywhere else. However, it proved uncharacteristic of the community—as warm and as opened-armed as you'll find anywhere.

A couple of other signs we saw in this general vicinity are worth repeating. One, a crayon lettered advertisement stapled to a fence post, let it be known that the upcoming farm had produce to spare. The sign, admirable for its Madison Avenue flair, began nobly enough but stubbed its toe at the end. It read, DELECTABLE ASPARAGUS FOR SAIL. Although we did not see it, few people pass through this area—famous for its fractured English—without hearing about the Pennsylvania Dutchman who had doorbell problems. Under the buzzer he placed the sign, BELL DON'T MAKE BUMP.

Another road sign we saw on the side of a barn was an enigmatic doubleheader—a two-in-one job that was so aged, its legibility suffered. Yet, one message was clearly evangelical in nature, admonishing sinners to repent, while the other recommended: TREAT YOURSELF TO MAIL POUCH TOBACCO. One sign had bled through and though I was not able to ascertain which came first, it made one wonder.

I never think of Mail Pouch, but what I remember my days spent as a grocery store delivery boy. That brand of chew tabacker was a mighty big favorite then, as I suppose it is today. People still chew, I guess, though with the exception of baseball players, I can't think who they might be. (I can still remember an interview I conducted during a recent World Series with one of major-league baseball's brightest luminaries. As he responded to my questions, tobacco juice oozed ever so daintily down his cheek creases.)

When I was delivering groceries there was a little old lady, a customer of the store, who chewed Mail Pouch—and was quite overt about it. I remember it was all right to deliver the chewing stuff without wrapping it, but with her Copenhagen snuff, that was another matter. She didn't want me unloading snuff on the kitchen table unless it was sacked and tied. As I recall, a sewing circle met at her house often and apparently she didn't think the girls would look as kindly on snuffin' as chawin'.

After a robust lunch of homemade bread, smearcase, chow-chow, corn-vegetable soup, shoofly pie and other Pennsylvania Dutch delicacies, we pedaled on westward from Lancaster to Columbia, across the historic Susquehanna and through Wrightsville on Route 30, stopping at some cabins just west of town. We had ridden forty miles, bringing our total to 175.

Our hosts that night were Ben and Naomi Zarfos, the first of several congenial husband-wife motel teams we encountered on the trip. After the kids were showered and bedded down, I went outside to unroll the tent that had been packed wet that morning. Mildew is something all experienced campers take steps to avoid, and I knew that unless I aired our tent that night, there was a strong possibility we would have fungus spots in the morning. Our other tent, a nine-by-fifteen umbrella model, bears the scars of mildew from two summers back.

Because the sky was overcast, I dragged the tent up on the porch of the cabin and rigged up a clothes line, over which to drape it. Unless a strong wind came with rain, chances were good it would be fairly dry by morning. Regardless, the airing would prevent mildew. While I was out doing my chores, Mr. Zarfos invited me to park the bikes in an unused garage up the way, and then after I had them under shelter, his wife shouted out their back door that the coffee was hot. They didn't need to call me twice.

Though I intended to make it a short cup, the Zarfoses had a whole bag of questions about our trip and we talked for better than two hours—until midnight. Not all the conversation was about bicycling, however. Playing reporter, I had some questions to ask them about operating a motel and they were full of experiences reflecting the noble and ignoble sides of people. When I finally finished my fourth cup of coffee and the last of the cookies, I bade them goodnight, suggesting they write a book about the motel business. I had the same comment for some other innkeepers on the trip, all of whom proved to be rather knowledgeable, tuned-in people.

Maybe it is because most of them have not been limited to a single work experience in their lives. As I recall, the motel business did not really get into high gear until after

World War II, which means that even the early birds in the trade are not much more than twenty-year veterans. Most motel people whom I met were more recent entrants. One fellow was retired from the State Patrol, another had been a top racing car driver, another a salesman and several had been farmers. One of our hosts was the cousin of the prominent California Democrat, Jesse Unruh.

Though none of the motel people I talked with would deny that the long hours and the confinement were disadvantages of the work, most seemed happy in their profession. I did jot down a couple of pet peeves that might be worth passing along: other than excessive noise, stolen towels and rubber checks, one of the most annoying impositions is the surreptitious way many guests smuggle pets into their rooms.

"We don't mind people taking their dogs inside if the animals are housebroken and don't scratch up the furniture," one motel keeper told me, "but I do think it looks a little ridiculous to see a grown woman carrying her poodle under her fur coat, trying to get it into the room without our seeing it."

Apparently, little goes unseen by motel owners. Invariably, they know when a couple is planning to stay less than a whole night. According to my informants, the scenes and dialogues follow a pattern.

Man drags himself into the motel office claiming great fatigue. He holds his head, his back or rubs his eyes. The woman stays in the car, often nestled far down in the collar of her coat, feigning sleep.

"Boy, are we tired," the man says with a sigh. "Been drivin' all day. All I want is a long sleep."

That is clue number one. The second giveaway is a line he often uses while registering. Normally, I understand, the next question concerns the price of the room, but Don Juan usually forgets to ask this one, and instead inquires: "What's checkout time?"

"Two hours later," one motel man said, throwing up his hands in disgust, "I look out the window and see the front door of their room wide open. Snow is blowing into it and every light in the place has been left burning."

June 12, Wednesday

> Late (8:30) start and weather threatening. Two or three miles down the road, rain began—a light sprinkle. We looked for shelter but before we found any it began pouring. . . .

That experience deserves some elaboration. Under a big tree, we held a poncho over our heads while Shirley sorted out rain gear from Steve's back basket, but by the time we got into pants and jackets it didn't matter. We were drenched. A new lesson: everyone should carry his own rain gear and, when threatening, keep it handy. We rode on, looking for a laundromat which we found at York (where Mad Anthony Wayne rallied troops for his march on Yorktown). We rallied behind washers and driers, changing out of soggy clothes into dry. The place was empty so it served nicely as a dressing room. Inside an hour, we were all repaired and ready to continue, but a newspaperman flagged us down and before we got out of town, we had our first bona fide interview. By the time we finished talking, it was time for lunch, so we didn't leave York until after one P.M.

With Gettysburg our goal, we set out again, but another downpour sent us for cover ten miles up the way. The metal awning of a rural appliance store saved us from another bath. Chris slept while we waited it out. About five o'clock we tried again, but a broken gear cable on Laraine's bike halted this thrust miles from anything. I had a spare cable in the tool bag, but didn't know if I'd have it fixed before dark. Surprisingly, I succeeded in a few minutes and we set out once again. Our frustrations weren't over though. About four miles short of Gettysburg, with both night and another storm moving in, my back tire began going soft. I didn't say anything to the rest, but kept riding, hoping we might be able to reach town before rim and pavement met. It didn't work out that way.

While I hurried through the tire repair procedure, darker clouds moved toward us and lightning cracked. A state patrolman stopped to ask if we needed help, but I assured him we were okay and he drove off, just as lightning crashed nearby. Chris' eyes stretched wide as baseballs. If he had been a little older, I think he would have called the patrolman back.

By the time I got the tire patched and remounted, it was dark and we rode, for the first time, after sunset, our lights making small punctures in the blackness. We quit at one of the first motels outside Gettysburg just as the rains came. Frustrated and bedraggled, we hurried into our room. In the whole day, we had come only 35 miles, 210 for the trip. Though we had expected to fall below 50 miles a day in the rugged belly of Pennsylvania, we had not yet reached the mountains, and we were already dropping way short.

June 13, Thursday

> Visited Gettysburg, a favorite place of ours from days gone by. We had agreed to stop long enough to see one attraction—a deal made earlier with Steve and Laraine. They chose the Wax Museum.

The Wax Museum proved a most interesting place with scores of Civil War personages caught in most realistic poses during significant moments in history. We all enjoyed the scenes except Chris, who was apprehensive of the "monsters."

He was more enthusiastic about the mechanical re-enactment (replete with rifle shots and cannon flashes) of such Gettysburg highpoints as Pickett's Charge and the Battle of Little Round Top. By way of explanation, all the action is set in a huge gymnasium-type room: spectators view the proceedings from raised bleachers. At their feet are soldiers in hand-to-hand skirmishes. They are surrounded by such battle props as raggedy tents, rearing horses, litter-bearing corpsmen, et al. On a speaker's platform near the rear of the room, Mr. Lincoln stands delivering his famous post-battle address with a passionate verve which brought tears to my eyes—I'm the sentimental type. It is an inspiring presentation, capable, I should imagine, of inducing patriotic palpitations in Ho Chi Minh, but just as Mr. Lincoln reached a forensic crescendo, Laraine dropped a metal pantleg guard, which went clanging down the concrete steps into the pit of bayonets and bandages. Fortunately, Mr. Lincoln is not one easily distracted, for he never paused, ". . . and that government of the people, by the people and for the people, shall not perish from the earth."

It was afternoon by the time we left Gettysburg on our way to Chambersburg, a much too auspicious projection. First, a strong wind came up, and it nearly blew us to a standstill, then Steve fell off his bike at a railroad crossing, scraping his knees, hands and pride. After first aid and a review of the proper method of riding across railroad tracks (at right angles), we continued. But by now Mount Newman, a climb for which we were not mentally prepared, was upon us and we began laboring upward. By the time we reached the top, we were too pooped to pedal on, so we coasted down to some cabins backed up by a rushing mountain stream. There we balmed our spirits, but the cyclometer told the bad news, 21 miles, 231 for our first week.

"And we're not even to the mountains!" lamented a discouraged Shirley.

Just then, Laraine and Steve came in the front door of the cabin leading Christopher at arm's distance much as if he were diseased or had been gunked by a skunk.

"Fresh tar," exclaimed Laraine.

And tar it was, from his sneezer to his sneakers.

I didn't have the heart to look full face at Shirley as I went out the door on my way for some gasoline. A peek over the shoulder was enough!

10 The Crash

The next day we reached the "real" mountains and if we had known then what the second week held for us, we would have swapped the bikes for Missouri mules.

The last spot to have made such a trade would have been Chambersburg, which we reached about ten thirty A.M. after a twelve-mile post-breakfast run. That was the morning of the fourteenth. There we bought lunch supplies, stopped at a cycle shop to get some spare gear cable (unavailable) and spent thirty minutes with a reporter.

While we were talking with the young woman from the local newspaper, several passersby saw the sign on the back of Chris' seat, THE BAUERS, PRINCETON, NEW JERSEY, and paused to ask where we were going. When we told them, their eyes shot wide like a scared Rochester in an old Jack Benny movie.

"Are there tigers out that way?" I laughed.

"Tuscarora," said one youngster.

"Anything like beriberi?"

"The mountain," he explained, thinking we didn't know that mountains lay ahead.

"You'll have to lead those bikes up 'em," said a man in overalls, who clinched an unlit pipe tightly between his teeth. "And if you get up 'em, you'll have to lead 'em down. Otherways, burn your brakes clean off."

"Ever know of anyone to ride Tuscarora on a bike?" I asked.

The man with the pipe shook his head no, and walked away. Captain Ahab had spoken. With such a solemn introduction, we were more than a little respectful of the terrain that stared down at us from the distance as we pedaled out of Chambersburg. But the mountains didn't stay in the distance. By three thirty—after lunch and a nap stop for Chris—we reached the foot of Tuscarora and the battle was joined.

As I said at the outset, in the first chapter, she was a formidable opponent, who nearly did us in. But we buoyed our spirits by singing, by counting off paces (50 at a time), by eating candy bars for energy and by taking frequent drinks from our limited water supply (two canteens, one quart each) and by resting wherever the road widened enough to pull off. One psychology lesson we learned in a hurry: pick short-term goals—the next tree or telephone pole. Never raise your eyes to the top, it's too discouraging.

By four thirty we had covered exactly one mile of the three-and-a-half. At that rate, I calculated we'd be lucky to reach the top (where there was a restaurant and a camping site) by dark—that is, if we kept going, and there was some question about that. The man in Chambersburg had said we would have to *lead* the bikes up the mountain. He was wrong. They wouldn't lead, but had to be pushed; and with the equipment we were carrying our backs complained more loudly as we progressed.

When five thirty came we were 2.1 miles up and one canteen down. By six, the second canteen was almost shot and we were looking for a campsite short of the top. It was about that time that the kids folded. "I can't go on," Steve said and when Laraine pulled up with a flat, she agreed. I let them stew while I repaired the tire. When finished, I posed this choice:

"If we stop short of the top, it's peanut butter sandwiches and no drinks; if we keep going it's T-bone steaks and iced lemonade."

About six thirty, we neared the three-mile mark and suddenly a service station sprung up on the left-hand side. Or was it a mirage? If so, we all saw a phantom Coke machine at once, for a new surge went through the troupe and we raced for a drink. After we had refreshed ourselves, we chatted with the owners of the station, Mr. and Mrs. Forester, I believe, inquiring about the facilities ahead.

"You'd be welcome to pitch your tent over there in the side yard," offered Mr. Forester. It was tempting.

At nearly seven o'clock, we had a half mile yet to go.

"Steaks and lemonade or peanut butter sandwiches and Cokes?" Weary bones outvoted appetites and we decided to stay.

After the tent was pitched, I wandered inside the gas station to ask Mr. Forester to fill our canteens. There, behind the counter I saw two things: a box of Hershey bars and a carton of red salmon.

"Do you sell groceries?" I inquired.

"Nope, but we do keep a few cans of salmon around. Need a can?" he asked.

"Well, now, that might go all right," I answered, trying to keep from drooling. "Sure, let me buy a can of salmon and a half dozen of those candy bars."

In a few minutes, we had our table set—on a grassy knoll covered with my poncho. For an appetizer we had hot soup; for the main course, sandwiches of salmon and peanut butter on Ritz crackers; for beverages, Cokes; and for dessert, chocolate bars. It wasn't Toots Shor's, but it wasn't bad.

June 15, Saturday

> We were fresh for the last half-mile climb, so it was a cakewalk and we were at the top for breakfast (pan-

cakes and sausage) by eight o'clock. After that, we whizzed down the other side, keeping an extra tight rein on the bikes, afraid a cable would snap or that "our brakes would burn clean off," as we had been warned. We moved through the valley past McConnellsburg and Harrisonville in good time and by three P.M. began our assault on Sideling Hill, which was about as long as Tuscarora.

This time we were a little better prepared for torture. The result was that Sideling (purportedly named by packers who with their horses had to sidle up the steep ridges) proved less of an ordeal than we had anticipated. One of the redeeming features of this climb was the water flows which trickled off rock formations near the road. Every third of a mile or so, we would stop to wash off our sweaty faces and take an icy drink—the water we had been told was perfectly safe at this altitude. We also found time to notice the view—a panorama of rolling countryside, chicly dressed in early summer green and newly opened wildflower accessories. The mountain laurel, tiger lilies, daisies, asters, violets and black-eyed Susans were in full glory. Birds and animals were also in abundance. Around one bend, we came upon a grazing doe and her weeks-old fawn, who both went scurrying through the woods with a clatter.

But the beauty of the place did not long distract us from our work. By the time we reached the top of Sideling, our legs felt like dangling rubber bands, and we were ready to take a chair. The roller coaster ride down cooled and refreshed us for a spell, but Ray's Hill was still between us and Breezewood, a Turnpike town where we hoped to find food and lodging.

By six o'clock we were laboring again and then to add to our difficulties, Chris—who had refused a nap earlier—decided it was time for a siesta. While he was sleeping, we surveyed the immediate vicinity for a place to camp, even though Breezewood could not be much further. But if it were only two miles, two miles uphill was more than we were prepared to undertake.

When Chris roused, we reluctantly set out again, ready to stop at any adequate site. Steve and Laraine crested the next rise first and there, let out a war whoop that would have frightened off Indians. When we caught up with them, we learned why. There at our feet basking in the setting sun was the town of Breezewood. We almost had stopped one hill too soon!

In a few minutes, we were in surroundings of luxury; the kids swimming in the motel pool, Shirley soaking in a tub of suds and I, spread-eagled, face down on the bed—the one nearest the door.

A little while later, we had the steaks we missed the night before.

June 16, Sunday

The cyclometer read 280 miles when we left Breezewood on our way to Everett, eight miles away. There we found a laundromat, our second wash stop of the trip. Had another newspaper interview, then set out for Bedford, seven miles ahead. We didn't make it—on bikes.

About one o'clock that afternoon, halfway between Everett and Bedford, we had a scare that we will never forget.

Though our normal riding order was myself, Steve, Laraine and Shirley, who served as a sort of mother hen in the rear, for some reason Laraine and Steve were out in front with Shirley and I following. We were observing normal safety procedures, riding single file to the extreme right side of the road.

Recreating the scene still gives me quivers, but I'll try, though we are not certain as to exactly what happened. We do know that we had just reached the top of a relatively steep grade and were all heading down when the accident occurred. As I was midway in the descent and Laraine was near the bottom, I had a good view of the crash. The first sign of danger was a sudden side-to-side waggle of her bike. Such a phenomenon is often caused, I'm told, by two factors: unequal weight distribution and speed.

When the bike began swaying, Laraine reacted properly, attempting to slow it down and regain control. However, she may have overreacted and applied her brakes too hard, especially the front caliper. When accelerating downhill most of a cyclist's weight is forward, leaving practically no drag at all on the rear wheel. With the center of gravity shifted so far forward, it takes very little front braking action to lift the back wheel off the ground and send it catapulting. Though I don't know positively, I believe Laraine may have reached for something in her front basket about the time the bike first wavered, leaving only one hand to steer and brake. If that one hand were her left, it would mean that she hit the front brakes only when her control problem developed. All of which is speculative and academic.

What I do know is that her front wheel turned ninety degrees against the direction the bike was moving and she flipped. In retrospect, it reminds me of one of those slow motion films of a steeplechase spill. First, the bike came to an abrupt stop. Next, the back wheel raised off the ground, sending Laraine forward—a horseback rider unseated. The back wheel became the one in front and Laraine twisted over, landing in a seated position with the bike draped over her.

To anyone who has ever been in such a helpless observing position, I don't have to describe the emotion that shot through Shirley and me. As I pedaled to Laraine, I remember issuing one of those instant prayers, "Oh, God, help her."

Arriving first, I leaned my bike against a guard rail, leaving Chris sitting at a precarious angle and ran to her. My initial concern was the traffic, which miraculously had not been bearing down upon us at the moment. I say miraculously because traffic was relatively heavy and Laraine had finished her spill in the middle of the right-hand lane. Already, cars were stopping in both directions, and when I got to her another man had parked his car on the left side and was coming across to help.

She was sitting up, not crying, but with a dazed look on her face.

"Are you all right?" I asked her. She didn't answer.

Lifting the bike from her, I could see several road burns on her legs. Her arms were also scraped and bloody, but her face and head were clean. Afraid she might have broken bones, I was reluctant to move her, but a motorist informed us that a county hospital was nearby and I knew a doctor should see her.

"Can you get up, Laraine?" I asked. By now, she had her wits about her, and said that she was all right.

Hobbling to a car, she was helped in and the motorist drove the two of us to the hospital's emergency entrance. By the time the doctor arrived in the emergency room, a nurse had cleaned all of her cuts and scrapes, including a raw burn on one hip, which was what concerned me most.

The doctor, after manipulating her leg, pronounced it unbroken. "You're a lucky girl," he winked. "But you'll be a little stiff for a few days, too stiff to ride a bike." The fact that we had ridden bicycles nearly 300 miles from our home was of special interest to hospital personnel, a number of whom had questions for us. One aide drove us back to the place where we had left the rest of the family, but Shirley, Steve and Chris were nowhere in sight. It had begun raining and they had taken cover. Driving up to the next farm, we found them, sheltered on the porch of the Floyd Smith residence. Mr. Smith further helped out by transporting us and our bikes into Bedford to a motel.

We had planned to sit out Monday anyway because I was scheduled to speak at a writer's conference in Philadelphia. I had planned to rent a car and drive back to

Philadelphia, but now, as I thought of Laraine's close call and surveyed her mangled front wheel, I wondered if we shouldn't all go back East, and call off this nonsense.

It was a question with which I wrestled all through that long half-awake, half-asleep night. Like an instant replay, I kept seeing one scene repeated; the back wheel of Laraine's bike flipping over in slow motion.

11 A Major Victory

Though Laraine put in a good night's sleep, she was indeed a sore, stiff-jointed gal the following morning. In addition to several dark bruises, the cuts and scrapes around her knees and elbows were even more angry-looking and any unnecessary motion caused her to grimace. She was certainly in no condition to ride a bike and, at that time, I could not imagine her ready for several days.

Yet we decided to put off any decision on the trip until Tuesday morning, after I had returned from Philadelphia.

Later that day, I rented a car, drove to the Turnpike and headed east. My only passenger was a pretzel-shaped front bike wheel which sat on the seat next to me, a silent reminder of Sunday's nightmare.

If we decided to continue, the wheel would need to be replaced and no bike shop in the Bedford vicinity had a spare. At Carlisle, I turned off the pike and hunted until I found a Schwinn shop where I bought a new wheel, as well as some spare gear cable for five-speed bikes.

After that I drove on to Philadelphia, spoke at the writer's conference and, about nine P.M., began driving back to Bedford, 200 miles away. I arrived at one A.M. Though everyone was asleep, Shirley woke up and we talked in whispers.

"How's Laraine?" I asked, looking over at her sleeping form.

"Much better," Shirley answered. "In fact, she went swimming in the motel pool."

"What!" I said out loud. Shirley shushed me and then repeated herself. It was hard to believe, but the next morning Laraine did a couple of restrained knee bends to prove she was okay, and ready to go on. I was still skeptical but took the wheel over to a bike shop, had it remounted and did a thorough check-over to see if anything else was amiss. Almost as amazing as Laraine's escape from serious injury was the fact that the bike was not a total wreck.

By eleven A.M. it was back together—and so were we, riding west again. A short distance out of Bedford, Laraine rode up close behind me to ask a question:

"Will I have any scars afterward, Dad?"

"No," I answered, "but your mother and I will."

For the rest of that week, we battled the last third of Pennsylvania, finishing off Laurel Hill, the final major obstacle, in the process. Though we continued to walk up some of the steeper inclines, our "bike hikes" became fewer and fewer. It was a combination of easier terrain and improved physical condition.

Our only adjustment following Laraine's accident was to show a little more restraint on descents. In the interest of safety, we sacrificed speed, even though it often created more work climbing the next rise. After her spill—without question—I took the lead on all downhillers and determined a safe speed. Laraine, in particular, used more caution than before. Despite a gradual leveling off of terrain, it was still anything but flat and we were unable to improve on our mileage. Each day there seemed to be some new drawback to delay us.

The day we resumed riding, we hit a horrible six-mile stretch of freshly plowed road, said to be under construction. It was in the vicinity of Manns Choice and West End, two communities on Route 31 which we took out of Napier. Actually, a detour was designated, but the road was open to local traffic and we decided to gamble. We lost.

With the exception of this one rough spell, however, our new route proved ideal for cycling—less traveled and much closer to nature. Then, too, it ran south of Pittsburgh, keeping us out of metropolitan traffic and lining us up more directly with Route 40 and Wheeling, West Virginia, two projected targets.

On Wednesday the 19th, rain parlayed with White Horse Mountain held us to 24 miles, duplicating the previous day's distance. The next day, a stiff head wind and Laurel Hill teamed up to stymie us as we fell to 20 miles, 360 for the trip. Friday, we rode 27 miles (despite two flats) and Saturday, just 17, spending half the day in Washington, Pennsylvania, at a bicycle shop. In truth, we were lucky to get Steve's *dérailleur* serviced at all as it was a Saturday afternoon and the shop was closed. However, I called the emergency number on the door and, upon hearing our story, a young man (named Joe Crawford) showed up to help us out.

It was typical of the kindness and generosity we kept receiving all along the way. Most everyone, it seemed, was willing to assist us. For example, Tuesday night of that week, we got hung up between towns and a family by the name of Welsh, east of Somerset, invited us to tent behind their grocery store, which we did.

It was a lucky break for us because our larder was low, and we were able to replenish our food supply at the store. Then, too, the camping was excellent. To provide grazing land for their pony, the Welshes had allowed the grass to grow lush and deep behind their barn, and it served as a wonderful mattress that night.

As I recall, the Welsh family had moved from Somerset to this little rural community, cozily nestled in a beautiful valley, a couple of years earlier. It was comparable to what Shirley and I had often talked of buying—a place in the country with a few acres of land and a pony for the kids.

I was surprised to learn that the Welshes were talking about returning to town. Though Mr. Welsh commuted daily to his job in town and the children rode the school bus, Mrs. Welsh was locked in place, tending the grocery store, and she missed the convenience of things in town. Hearing them discuss the pros and cons of the pastoral life made us do a double-take.

"Maybe we'd want to reverse field after a year or two, too," said Shirley.

"Would you like living on a farm?" I asked Steve and Laraine.

"Not me," fired Laraine.

"Me neither," said Steve.

"Well, when we find our farm," I told Shirley, "we can forget the pony."

Later that week, the night after we camped in beautiful Kooser State Park, we got into another bind and again some friendly folks came to our rescue, though for a while, it looked as if we might spend the night on bikes. As before, we had got caught short of a town with motel or camping facilities, so we were forced to scrounge for a place to sleep. Though I am sure this predicament sounds abominable to travelers accustomed to firm reservations, we faced such problems over and over again on the trip, and it became something of a game. A game which requires a spirit of adventure and resourcefulness.

On this particular occasion, we reached a little community south of Pittsburgh named Ginger Hill. We were too bushed to go on and night was not far off, so we thought it time to begin our search. First, I inquired at a bar, usually about the friendliest place around for strangers, but this time I drew a blank. Though sympathetic, neither proprietor nor customers were able to make any valid suggestions.

Outside, I was greeted by a loud hissing noise coming from the direction of my bicycle. Investigating, I found that the air was escaping from my back tire and, there before my wide eyes, Christopher settled lower and lower. I knew it was not the time to fix a flat; our immediate need was a place to pitch a tent, so I walked down the way, knocking on several doors. I got nowhere.

"Let's forget this place," I told Shirley. She gave me a weary "no room at the inn" look and I answered with a "what am I supposed to do?" shrug. Just then, up the way, a boy rode a horse out of a farmyard onto the highway. Where there is a horse, there must be a barn, I figured, so we walked toward the farm. The kids had talked about spending a night in a hay mow. This might be their chance.

Down the road we walked, me pushing a crippled bike that went *kurop, kurop, kurop* every time the back tire went around. Finally, we reached the farm and there I told my story to Mr. and Mrs. Dick Kovacs, who warmly took us in. Though they had just a shed for the horse, there was plenty of room for a tent. While I was pitching it, Mrs. Kovacs invited Shirley to prepare supper over her stove and in minutes we had been fed.

Later that night, we were asked in for Cokes (Dick is a delivery man for the company), popcorn and TV. In exchange for stories about our trip, we got a tour of the house which they were remodeling. The conversation lasted way beyond our bedtime, but it was fast-paced and exhilarating. By the time we went to our tent, it seemed as if the Kovacs were people we'd known all our lives.

The next day, Sunday noon, June 23, we reached the Pennsylvania-West Virginia line. By way of celebrating, we bought an ice cold watermelon. Victory!

We had come 419 miles (364 across Pennsylvania) in seventeen days. Actually, it had taken us less than that by adjusted time. Pennsylvania, I figured, consumed about twelve days of actual riding. But whatever the distance, we were at least 200 miles behind schedule, and needed a rally to recoup our deficit.

After Pennsylvania, we were anxious to try Beautiful Ohio, beautiful, flat Ohio.

12 Freewheeling Through Ohio

In my native state, the State of Presidents (by virtue
of quantity if not quality), cycling began to become the
joy it is reputed to be. Fortunately, we had more than
two weeks in which to discover the fun; otherwise the
Bicycling Bauers (an alliteration too tempting to pass up
for most newspapermen) might have quit this new
masochism, impaled upon one of Pennsylvania's untouted
peaks.

All the while we had been involved in the gruelling
climbs, I was aware of an unspoken anxiety which rode

with us. It was brought on, I suppose, by a number of factors—mechanical difficulty with the bikes, physical fatigue, the traffic and probably most prominent, the haunting question of whether or not we could really make it through Pennsylvania.

I first observed this anxiety subtly interwoven in the perseverance of Laraine and Steve. Though there were many times in the mountains when they were hurting— exhausted and depressed enough to throw in the towel— they could not in fact have been dragged from their bikes. The reason was a simple matter of pride. They had made a commitment to their friends ("We are going to ride our bikes to California") and now they must do it. To return home after 200 miles would have been more shame than wearing blue sneakers to gym class!

But once we had cleared our first major obstacle, new confidence, new strength, new poise oozed from both of them. Whatever happened after that, at least they could claim Pennsylvania as a cycling trophy. Steve and Laraine were particularly amused when I passed along the news that some of the folks back home had wagered against our making it to Ohio. I learned of the speculative interest in our trip when I called my secretary, Ellie Sass, one day shortly after we had reached the Buckeye State.

"And," Ellie told me, her natural enthusiasm bubbling, "if you keep going, some more money is going to change hands." When I asked her how she was betting, she answered, "Just keep pedaling."

"Tell me, what are the odds on us making it to the Mississippi?" I inquired.

"Way down since we learned you were free of Pennsylvania."

Before I could suggest that I might like in on the action, my three minutes ran out. When I told Shirley, she had a cruel putdown: "Which way would you have bet?"

Ellie had used the phrase, "free of Pennsylvania," and free was the right word, for suddenly we felt released, as if we had been propelled into Ohio by a giant slingshot—the terrain improved that much. And each day that we rode deeper into the bowels of America, the feeling of total freedom—a joyous abandon, a kind of relaxed rhythm—grew. Anne Morrow Lindbergh, in her beautiful classic, *Gift from the Sea,* talks about this feeling as she described her second week at the shore: "One becomes like the element on which one lies, flattened by the sea; bare, open, empty as the beach, erased by today's tides of all yesterday's scribblings."

That erasing process had been completed for me by the end of the third week. Up until then, I think I was physically astride a bicycle; mentally, I was home doing my work. I can imagine a psychiatrist saying that my puritan work ethic had held me captive and, being chock full of guilt, I was unable to savor the experience. If one were to make such an assessment, I think I would be inclined to agree. For, face it, most men find it threatening to leave their jobs for even a two-week vacation.

"How will the company get along without me?" is an unspoken question most male animals pose to themselves, and I'm certain legions refuse vacations each year in fear the company may learn the answer. Anyway, the day-to-day tension that grips most families vanished for us, and suddenly we were free to enjoy our ten-week lark. There were no phones to answer, no deadlines to meet, no meetings to attend, no trains to catch and no loyalty tests between work and family. All there was was bicycle riding—simple, uncomplicated, uncerebral.

Harmony. All of our efforts were bent in one direction, a novelty for any family with children over ten. To have a successful day, we had only a few basic requisites— properly functioning bikes, healthy bodies, plenty of energy-producing food and a place to sleep. (We even survived in the main without TV.) In regard to food and sleep, I can say without equivocation that food had never tasted better and sleep was never more welcomed.

Such a simplistic daily discipline brought with it a satisfaction, a peace, a tranquility, unexperienced since boyhood. Suddenly, our senses were pricked awake and we became mobile aesthetes, all of us, appreciative of a fanning maple's shade, a mockingbird's ecstatic song, the taste of dead-ripe blackberries picked from a roadside bush, the afterglow of a sunset.

Each day became an entity in itself—*finis, pau, fait accompli*. So unlike so many of the no-victory, no-defeat days which make up much of adult life. Those days we play in the shadowy cracks of the piano, seldom venturing to make music or seldom striking a single ivory key unless we do it on cue after a poll has been taken of the players, who then hit a consensus note—in unison.

As a writer, I am well acquainted with this amalgama-

tion syndrome from which this identity-seeking generation has become sick and rebelled. Maybe it has been a
part of life, always, but I cannot help but believe the
frustration more pronounced now. I have often eyed with
no little envy the baseball player who takes the field before the crowds each day. He does his job, takes a shower
and exits, knowing full well whether or not his team won
or lost and knowing full well what he contributed to that
outcome—plus or minus. Furthermore, the next morning's
paper recounts his previous day's output in black and
white. The box score—cold, factual, uncolored—reports
his hits, his runs, his errors.

In bicycling, we discovered a parallel, a therapy for
tired bodies responding to tired minds, too long shackled
by routine, inconclusive endeavors. And in an age hung
up on tranquilizers and pep pills (as well as stronger
substances), that's no minor discovery.

June 23, Sunday

. . . After reaching the West Virginia line, we rode
trough-like Route 40, the old National Highway, into
Wheeling in a breeze. Took time out for Chris' nap
(in an Isaly's ice cream store booth) and then walked
our bikes to the top of McCulloch's Leap. (This is
where Scout McCulloch allegedly escaped his Indian
pursuers by riding horseback down an embankment
which would rival the face side of Mount Rushmore.)
Steve was impressed but had one question: Did he
live? Wheeling behind us, we crossed the Ohio River
and called it a day at Bridgeport, Ohio. 35 miles, 439
total.

How Many Hills to Hillsboro?

June 24, Monday

Took Route 40 through St. Clairsville to Hendrysburg where our road suddenly deserted us. Interstate 70 had swallowed it up and we were left to weave through the backwoods on unpaved county roads until Route 40 resumed at Old Washington. Though the detour cost plenty of time, it was beautiful country, alive with birds and animals. Furthermore, we were lucky not to be traveling a more circuitous route. Had we listened to a state patrolman, and not a local resident, we would have gone another 30 miles out of our way. But it was a day of conflicting information. Rain was not in the forecast, but we got caught in a downpour. Toward evening, we were directed to a motel which had been closed a year and then to an "open all evening" grocery which closed at six. In the end, we camped at an overnight trailer spot, improvising a meal out of a Mother Hubbard cupboard. Got more rain during the night. 33 miles, 472 total.

June 25, Tuesday

We awoke early (from hunger no doubt) and quickly went foraging for breakfast. Chased a dairy truck servicing a little community east of Old Washington, hoping for a quart of orange juice, but we lost the race. Out of breath, we rested in the driveway of a tavern, drawing the interest of the owner who invited us in to eat. A tavern which opened at 7 A.M. was a new one on me, but we had a jim-dandy meal. For entertainment, an old-timer sitting at the bar told about his boyhood in Wyoming, claiming to have been on cattle drives with Buffalo Bill Cody. (Steve would have stayed to listen all day.) After haircuts, a laundromat stop, a grocery visit and lunch in Cambridge, we set out for Zanesville, as carefree as Little Red Riding Hood. We ran into our "wolf" at New Concord, the birthplace of John Glenn.

Fighting a running skirmish with the weather all day, we finally found sunshine as we neared New Concord and put away our rain gear—for a spell. But after a soda break, the clouds were back again, and just as we climbed on our bikes, the sky dumped a torrent of rain on us. It was a duplication of our earlier experience outside Wrightsville in Pennsylvania. Before we could get into our gear or take cover, we were drenched to the insteps of our socks. Finally, in fear of being drowned, we made a run for an open garage up the way. Though I doubt the cycling manual recommends taking refuge in strange garages, this was an emergency. And anyway, we didn't really go all the way in, but rather sat on our bikes just inside the doorway.

There, we got reorganized, dried off and changed and prepared to continue—but a curtain of rain held us inside the garage. Finally, it stopped as abruptly as it had begun. At the same time, the wind quit as if a fan had been turned off. In fact, it was ethereally quiet.

"Look," said Shirley, pointing toward the hill directly in front of us. "It's a tornado!"

And it was, a coal black funnel not half a mile away, whirling wildly across a wan, anemic-looking sky. Lined up on bikes ready to push off, we froze at the garage entrance, not saying a word. At the outer edge of the dervish, debris could be seen trailing the main funnel. First, these materials were thrown free of the cone and then after a second's suspension, they would be sucked back into the turbulence and spun again. It reminded me of that carnival ride—the tilt-o-whirl, I believe—with its spinning cars which revolve on an undulating, circular track.

Across the horizon the twister slowly moved, eliminating a first fear I had had that it was coming toward us. In a matter of seconds, the funnel passed from left to right and was gone. Steve was the first to break the silence, delivering his strongest expletive:

"Wow!"

Then, with mock fright (I think it was mock) he said, "Let's get out of here."

As we were heading in the opposite direction toward Zanesville, it seemed like an excellent suggestion, and off we rode. But we had more excitement ahead. Twice in the next ten miles we were lashed by sudden rain squalls, causing us to search the ominous sky for more twisters. Each time, I wondered about the wisdom of leaving New Concord, but we pushed on. Finally, the sun emerged, but this signaled for more wind and within a few miles we found it almost impossible to pedal.

"Let's find a motel," I shouted back at Shirley, who was riding twenty-five yards behind me, bent low to cut resistance. Her answer was, "Fine," though I had to read her lips, for not a trace of her voice penetrated the blast.

About fifteen minutes later at five thirty, we reached

a motel and sighed in relief, but inside I learned there was no vacancy.

"How far to the next motel?" I asked.

"About a mile," the proprietor answered. I turned to leave, but stopped in mid-pirouette. The TV program being broadcast in the lobby had been interrupted for a weather bulletin—a tornado alert.

Outside, I told the others that we'd need to pedal another half mile—a mile sounded impossible in that wind —but I told them nothing about the news I had heard on TV. One problem at a time.

Finally, we struggled into the next lodge, a group of cabins, and this time we were accommodated. After unloading, we all slumped down on the beds exhausted. Our eyes were heavy from the buffeting of the wind, like after a day at the beach. When we went up the road for supper, the wind was still blowing, and was the subject of conversation at the restaurant.

". . . And the tornado blew a truck off Route 40 just east of New Concord about three thirty," one man at the next table said. Shirley buried her face in her hands, peeking out at me from between her fingers. She was thinking what I was thinking. We had been on Route 40, east of New Concord about three o'clock. The tornado had missed five bicyclists by half an hour!

About nine o'clock, we returned to our quarters and climbed into bed. Though the wind was still blowing at a good fifty miles an hour, we determined not to let it keep us from sleep. And it didn't—for a while.

About ten thirty, one of the swinging windows in the little crackerbox cottage banged loudly against the wall, causing Shirley and me to bolt upright at the same time, much as Will Stockdale's wired toilet seats in *No Time For Sergeants*.

"It's coming," said Shirley, an eerie quality to her voice. Judging from the increased wind velocity, "it" was indeed.

"Don't get excited," I calmed, trying not to choke on my words. All I could think about was an experience we had had a few years earlier at Hamilton, Indiana, at my parents' lake cottage. It is also a small frame structure, surrounded by equally mammoth trees. When they creak and groan in the wind, one can imagine—with no difficulty at all—what would be left of the cottage if a tree were to come down. One night an eighty-mile-an-hour wind blew through that lake community, sending its residents into all forms of panic. One of them, whose safety always has interested me, took cover under a roll-away bed until danger passed.

Well, I didn't get under a bed this night, but the thought crossed my mind. Instead, I sought relief from the radio, an old box not far from the crystal set era, which sat on the bureau. However, all I could draw from it were whines and squeals.

"Turn it down," Shirley said in a stage whisper. "You'll wake the kids." That seemed unlikely. They had snoozed through all the noise outside with nary a turn-over. Finally, I centered the dial on the loudest squeal where, between oscillations, I could hear Guy Lombardo music incongruously vying with the tornado. Then the announcer came on: "Just to repeat an earlier announcement, the weather bureau . . . Rurrwaru . . . all clear . . . Nuuuwarooo . . . effective eleven o'clock. . . ." I held my watch up to the light coming from the radio dial —eleven fifteen.

"Well, there, sweetheart, we can go back to sleep," I reassured.

Just then, a large limb gave way somewhere nearby and went crashing to the ground. Shirley jumped toward me, her arms flailing. One caught me across the nose. Surprisingly, the punch did not draw blood, so she was only penalized one yard to her side of the bed and we went back to sleep.

June 26, Wednesday

> Made bike adjustments at Schwinn shop in Zanesville (Steve Lindsay, the proprietor, particularly helpful.) Interviewed by Zanesville newspaperman. Reporter and photographer especially interested in a new passenger we had acquired, a turtle (the first of three) christened Uncle Louie by Steve. Louie came aboard at Washington, Pennsylvania. A short way out of town, we were stopped again by newspaper people. They had decided to do a full-page spread on family cycling and needed more pictures. We were running late and were reluctant to give up more time, but a birthday cake melted us.
>
> Steve and Chris, who had had birthday parties before the trip, officially turned 11 and 3 on June 25 and June 26. Learning this, the reporters decided to pre-

sent them with a cake, which served nicely as a prop for more photographs. Finally, we got on our way, reaching Newark by dinner time. My sister and brother-in-law, Joy and Wayne Bulla of Westerville, met us there and transported us to their house for the night. We returned to Newark the next morning and rode Route 161 to Route 3, north of Columbus. We stayed with the Bullas again that night.

June 28, Friday

The start of our third week, 568 miles along. Traffic heavy and difficult head wind, but made 36 miles to Mechanicsburgh, northeast of Springfield. Stayed at a tourist home.

June 29, Saturday

Wind down, but heat up to over 90. All had some salt pills. Nonetheless, road good, terrain flat. Rode 44 miles, stopping at Vandalia, northwest of Dayton. Best mileage since early in the trip. Our total now stands at 648.

June 30, Sunday

Our goal this day was a 50-mile ride, which we figured would carry us into Indiana. Well, we made Indiana all right, but fell four miles short of our projection. We were lucky to make 46. Had we not fought a bridge-out detour, we might have spent the night in Ohio. "Any possibility we could ford the stream?" I asked a mechanic. "Sure," he answered, "it's shallow and sandy bottomed." Shirley was skeptical, but we decided to try.

We went around the detour sign, and three miles later we reached the stanchions marking the end of the line. There was only one problem: wire was strung from the barriers in the middle of the road all the way over to the fences and there was no access to the river's bank. It was no go. When I announced we had been given a bum steer and would have to retrace our tracks, there were groans all around.

"Well, you win some and lose some," Mother consoled.

"Let's rest a minute," begged Steve, who had spotted a fruit-laden mulberry tree along the road. While the rest ate berries, I made one last survey, going down into a culvert to investigate the barbed wire fence. To my surprise, I discovered that a single strand of baling wire stood between us and the creek. It was a simple matter to unwrap it, and in a minute I was at the water's edge. It was unnecessary to wade across, because the construction men had made a fill to enable trucks to cross back and forth with their loads. There was a problem on the other side, however: getting out. Fencing was strung across the road in the same manner. Then, I noticed a path off toward a pasture. Following it, I walked into an open field—road and fence on one hand, a woods on the other. I was sure a big black Angus bull was about to charge from the foliage, but none did and I soon found the gate leading out of the field. It was a swinging gate, closed by a simple wire loop.

Inside of five minutes I had ushered the family down to the river, over the fill, across the field and out on the highway again. After securing the fences, we were soon racing on to Richmond, proud of our ingenuity, though Steve was somewhat disappointed.

"We didn't really ford a river, did we?"

"No, but we may have to the next time," I answered. That seemed to satisfy him, but not Shirley. She began whistling "Show Me the Way to Go Home."

13 Dream Country

All along the way—and our next state, Indiana, was no exception—we kept encountering people who seemed to get a vicarious charge out of our caravan on wheels. Though we expected to be viewed as vagabond kooks, few greeted us with anything but warm inquisitiveness. Most abounded in questions.

"You mean you've ridden those things all the way from New York City?"

"Don't you get tired?"

"Where do you eat . . . sleep?"

"Isn't it dangerous?"

"How far are you going?"

"Why are you doing it?"

"How many miles do you make a day?"

"How old is the little one?" And on and on.

Of course, there were some who just gawked, saying nothing, but speaking tons with their faces. Scrooge-like, they were puckered into "bah, humbug" smirks. Yet seldom did their cynicism turn vocal. An exception was in a small Ohio town outside a restaurant.

We had just eaten and were preparing to mount our horses when a man staggered out of a bar next door and measured us with watery eyes. Weaving like a fighter in the ring, he composed himself enough to shoot out an index finger at me and state:

"Tom inside says you guys rode bikes all the way from New York. I told him I had five dollars that said he was full of. . . ." (I motioned the others to ride on ahead.) After I confirmed the story, he bellowed: "What's wrong with the pack of you? Are you out of your mind?"

"The jury's still out," I answered. "Have you ever ridden a bike?"

"Yes, but not halfway across the country. You don't think I'm that crazy, do you?"

"I haven't known you long enough to make a valid judgment," I told him and rode off.

But, by and large, we were queried by people who were genuinely interested in our kind of adventure. At heart, we discovered, almost everyone has a deep-seated longing to escape his present routine, and to embark on some romantic undertaking. To sail away across oceans, to fly to distant, exotic countries, to explore, to discover. As could be expected, these pangs burn most fervently in the hearts of those who have done most of their traveling, like Henry David Thoreau, in "Concord."

There were some who had made unforgettable forays, mostly in their long-ago youth, and they shared these experiences with nostalgic passion.

"When I was seventeen," one gent reminisced, his false teeth clicking as he talked, "I rode a horse all the way to St. Louis." Another remembered the thrill of traveling with the circus for a few months, "much against my Pappy's wishin'." A gray-haired woman, her face creased with happy wrinkles—the kind which turn up—recalled with pride, the Spartan summer trip her family made by Model T to Denver. "There weren't any motels in those days and we camped most nights by rivers."

When I heard anecdotes such as these I couldn't help thinking of a scene in the movie, *National Velvet*. (Yes, it was a talkie, kids.) As I recall, Liz Taylor, a teen-ager no less, had given up on the idea of entering her pet horse in the big race, the Grand National, because she didn't have money enough for the entry fee. Her heart was broken. But Mother or Stepmother (in such a tearjerker I suppose her mother had died) comes through in the clutch and provides the cash. The reason she gives is that once in everyone's life, there comes a moment too big to be missed.

Apparently, many people miss that moment, judging

from the stories I heard on the trip. One cherubic-looking man with white cotton balls of hair around his ears confided: "I always wanted to take a steamer around the world, but it never worked out." He shared his dormant dream self-consciously, not sure whether he should pass it off as a joke or a serious intention.

"Why didn't you?" I asked.

"Oh, Dad needed lots of help on the farm . . . and then I met Doris . . . marriage . . . children . . . responsibilities."

"Why don't you go on that trip now?"

"No, I couldn't, or shouldn't. Never know when a rainy day will come along. I've got a house, a little savings, but I don't ever want to become a burden on my kids. Anyway, I'm too old to travel. Wouldn't enjoy it. I get ten miles away from home and begin getting fidgety. But now, if I were a mite younger, I'd go along with you. . . ."

He laughed. I laughed, not saying what I was thinking. It would have been contradictory, for he wouldn't be going along with us anymore than going on a steamer trip. It wasn't in his genes. He is a conservative, practical man today, as he was yesterday. So was his father, I imagine. They had heard the same bluebird whisper temptingly to come join the fun, to take a chance, loosen up; but the pressures of tradition, fear of failing, of looking silly, had caused them to shoo the bird away, just as most of us do. Yet, some rare individuals break ranks, as in a little quatrain I once wrote:

Like mechanized carnival ducks
We move along a pre-set track,
But occasionally, one discovers wings
And flies off, never to come back.

The very first night we spent in Indiana, seven miles
west of Richmond at Twin Lake Recreation Park, we met
a man who was working on a dream. In fact, it was in
part, a reality. Mr. Duff was his name. His dream: to
take a twenty-five-acre woods and turn it into a camping-
fishing-swimming-picnicking facility. And he has done it.
With bulldozers, basins were carved for lakes; and they
were stocked with fish. Camping sites were staked out,
sand transported in for swimming and sunning, roads
made. It is far from completed, Mr. Duff admitted, but
it is a huge asset to the community, one that I can
imagine is greatly appreciated or should be.

But what I remember most about my conversation
with Mr. Duff is another statement: "I've had a barrel of
fun doing it and, though it will take ages to break even,
I wouldn't give up the experience for anything. Then,
too, I think my grandchildren will enjoy it."

Mr. Duff is a man after my own heart, as was another
Hoosier I met up the way. Well, I didn't really meet him;
he wasn't around when I visited his home. The man's
name: James Whitcomb Riley of Greenfield, Indiana.
Yes, the poet, who has been gone for better than fifty
years, but has the immortality of a successful writer.

When we passed through Greenfield, it was a scorching
hot day and the family took time out for rest and refresh-

ment while I visited the Riley homestead. It was a worth-while respite, immersing myself once again in the Hoosier dialogue of the man who gave us:

Little Orphant Annie

An' the Gobble-uns'll git you
Ef you don't watch out.

The Raggedy Man

O', the Raggedy Man he works fer Pa,
An' he's the goodest man ever you saw!

When the Frost Is on the Punkin

A pictur' that no painter has the colorin' to mock—
When the frost is on the punkin and the fodder's in the shock.

The Man in the Moon

There's a boil on his ear and a corn on his chin—
He calls it a dimple—but dimples stick in.

Like Mr. Duff, Riley lived long enough to see his dream blossom, for by the turn of the century he was probably the nation's wealthiest, most beloved and best-known poet—exonerated from his father's charge that he would never amount to anything. Riley senior, a lawyer, had apparently brought considerable pressure on his son to forget poetry and embark on a more utilitarian work, but his son held to his dream and we are the richer for it.

When we reached the Indiana line and Richmond on Sunday, June 30, we had completed a 271-mile trek across the Buckeye State in a week, our best period to date. We were still below the 300-mile-a-week pace we had hoped for, but we were gaining. After the first 100 miles in southeast Ohio, the last of the Allegheny Plateau, we reached what is topographically called the Central Lowlands, a strip of relatively flat terrain that stretches for nearly 450 miles to the Mississippi River. Midway through Ohio, our mileage began to pick up and the improvement carried over into Indiana.

Following Route 40, we had our first fifty-mile day, on the nose, on July 1. It brought us to 744 miles and Cumberland, just west of Indianapolis. In the course of this day's riding, we bisected Route 3, which runs north-south between Louisville, Kentucky, and Fort Wayne, Indiana. It may run farther, but its significance for me is that it was the highway I often hitchhiked while I was in the Army at Fort Knox.

What memories Route 3 brought to the surface! I don't know what the record is for three-day passes during basic training, but I claim it, until challenged. In sixteen weeks, I made the 700-mile round trip between Fort Knox and Bryan, Ohio (where Shirley, pregnant with Laraine, was staying with her folks), a total of fourteen times. Because I didn't have money for bus fare and because a bus took longer, I hitchhiked most of the trips, leaving Friday night and arriving back in time for five o'clock reveille Monday morning.

How was I able to obtain so many passes? By volunteering to help the company clerk. When our morning report specialist learned I could type, he turned the whole orderly room over to me and set up his office at the PX bar, leaving me in charge of passes. Very poor judgment.

Fortunately, basic training lasted only sixteen weeks and the Army shipped me off to Hawaii, otherwise I don't think I would have survived much longer. After one of those sleepless weekends, it took three days to recuperate for the next three-day pass.

After Cumberland and a rough battle with Route 40 traffic for a while, we turned south and bypassed Indianapolis, picking up Route 42 to Monrovia. This was the first time I'd been near Indianapolis since my last trip with Dad to the "500." The Indianapolis 500 is another one of those memory launchers, because when I was younger, we made the trip to the races every year for several in a row. Though occasionally Mother, my brother Bob or sister Joy would go along, often, it was just Dad and me. We would leave about midnight, the day of the race, and drive to Speedway City, arriving about dawn. The idea was to beat the traffic. Once there, we'd sleep in the car until breakfast, after which we'd go to the grandstand and watch the race preparation, almost as exciting as the race itself. By the time we got home, it was dark again, and we were both so tired we could hardly crawl out of the car, but it is one of those father-and-son experiences that warms me inside when I think about it today.

The only comparable event during my boyhood was our annual trip to Detroit and Briggs Stadium (Mr. Briggs' name has been dropped I know, but it will always be Briggs Stadium to me). Dad would make elaborate preparations for that day, though I suspect it was in part to heighten my anticipation. Still it took some arranging. For one thing, he worked at a lumberyard, and the game required him to lay off a day. That scheduled, he had to order tickets, always the most expensive.

"We'll get first base box seats," he would say every year, as regular as the Fourth of July. "They cost a little more, but when you go as seldom as we do, I think we should have the best. Right, Joe?" (He always called me by my middle name, I suppose, because his dad's name was Fred.) When the momentous day approached, we would study the weather forecast and if there was even an outside chance of rain, I would pray for all I was worth. And my prayers were pretty powerful in those days, for I don't think we ever had to take a rain-check. It would have been catastrophic, of course, because Dad wouldn't have been able to lay off two days in a row, and I would have missed seeing the Yankees and the Tigers that year. (I was a Yankee fan long before I came East.)

On the big day, we would drive the 150 miles to Detroit and arrive at the stadium in plenty of time to see batting practice. We didn't want to miss any part of the show. During the course of the game, Dad spent as much of his time waving at hawkers, replenishing our peanut and pop supply as he did watching the game. "Baseball is not baseball without peanuts," he would say, sticking an elbow in my ribs and winking. To this day, I can't watch a ball game without a sack of peanuts.

Continuing our bypass of Indianapolis on Route 42 we reached Monrovia, a little town north of Bloomington by mid-afternoon. There, a service station attendant suggested we might want to ride Route 70, north of town. It was completed, he explained, but not yet open to traffic. We decided to chance it.

The new road was as smooth as glass and the limited traffic made it ideal for cycling, though the wind was a negative factor. Also, we were somewhat bothered by the shortage of exits, several miles apart. Nonetheless, we stayed on Route 70 till we reached Cloverdale, about seven o'clock. Though we could tell from our maps that it was not a large town, we hoped to find food and a place to camp. We were in luck.

Thoroughly exhausted after sixty miles of cycling (our best day), we pulled into a drive-in restaurant on the north edge of town. There we met Jack Swope and his wife, the owners of the place.

First, we talked with his wife, who took our order and then, from where I don't know, Jack showed up. A tall, athletic-looking guy of forty-plus, he wore that midwest rarity—a beard. I had threatened to skip shaving on the trip, but Shirley wouldn't let me. "Out here, many consider long hair or a beard the mark of a hippie," she had advised, and remembering my attitudes about those things a few years earlier, I had to agree. If we needed help, it would not be to our advantage to have a bushy-chinned leader, we concluded.

But now, here came Jack—full-bearded on a motorcycle. Both he and his wife were enthusiastic about our venture, and shared some of their interests—traveling, motorcycling (they once rode to Florida on one in the dead of winter), camping, skiing and parachuting. Yes, parachuting. Jack is a sky diver who belongs to a club and performs regularly at fairs and special celebrations. While I was still open-mouthed from that news, he began telling me about a trip he had taken into Central America a few years earlier by motorcycle. He and a friend rode on cycles until mechanical problems forced them to go on by foot—somewhere in Costa Rica as I recall. Then they ran into a small-scale war, and were arrested by one of the warring factions, charged with being American mercenaries. It was an understandable conclusion, because Jack and his friend were armed to the teeth with guns and knives, though they intended to use them for hunting, not fighting.

Actually, they were happy to be captured because, after their motorcycles quit on them, they had become lost in the jungles and for several days went without eating. To keep from starving they turned to iguanas, which were horrible tasting, according to Jack.

"That is until we learned we were shooting the wrong kind," he recalls. "We were eating large males, but later learned that the small females are tastier." Look that up in your Funk and Wagnall's.

In the end, the State Department intervened and arranged for the two American adventurers' release, but not any too soon, I understand.

When I asked Jack where he would suggest we camp that night, he led us to his place, directly behind the

restaurant. What a beautiful layout. Not only the sprawl-
ing ultramodern home, which Jack had built mostly by
himself, but the landscaping which included three man-
made lakes. We camped beside one of the lakes after we
had spent the better part of the evening looking at the
Swopes' family album and sharing opinions about a thousand and one subjects. In almost every instance, Jack
had a little something fresh and original about his attitudes.

Shirley and I found the Swopes people in love with
life, full of zest for it, excited about it and 100 percent
tuned in. When Jack told me of all the business ventures
he is in, I asked how he found time for his extracurricular
interests. "I take time," he laughed. "If there is no time
to enjoy things as you go along, then you're too busy.
What good is a pile of money when you're an old man?"

The next morning, July 3, we awoke, surrounded by a
milky fog that hung low over the lakes and dewy pas-
tures. The sun trying to break through created little rain-
bow prisms wherever one looked. As we loaded our bikes
and rode off, one of Jack's horses came running along a
fence through the mist, whinnying loudly.

"I think she wants to come along," Shirley called over
from her bike.

"Tell her she's already in Camelot," I shouted back.

14 A Long Detour

July 3, Wednesday

> Followed Route 42 through Cunot, past scenic Cataract Lake and Poland toward Terre Haute, but mid-morning we hit a new snag: sickness.

The first clue that Chris was not feeling well came at breakfast when he ate very little, but first evidence that he was really ill came after we had been on the road a little over an hour. I heard him whimpering and stopped the bike to see what was wrong.

"I want down," he told me. Shirley pulled up beside me as I parked the bike, unfastened his safety belt and lifted him out of his seat.

"What's wrong?" she asked. Chris answered by up-chucking what little he had had for breakfast, the first sickness we had had in nearly four weeks of riding. Though we all had been drenched several times, had ridden through wilting heat and chilling wind, no one had developed even a case of the sniffles until then. Amazing, but true.

Shirley checked Chris' forehead and announced that he had a slight fever. His flushed cheeks further testified that he was hot, so we stowed the bikes along the road, found an inviting tree, laid a poncho under it and placed Chris on it (with his security blanket). After a search Shirley found the aspirins in the first aid kit which contained everything from a snakebite tube to salt tablets. She gave Chris half a pill with some water and he was soon asleep. As she recapped the canteen, I suggested that maybe his upset stomach was brought on by so many changes of water, but none of the rest of us had been bothered, so that seemed unlikely.

Just what we were going to do when he woke up was anyone's guess. We were miles from the nearest town and a doctor, if he needed one. Suddenly I had a new appreciation for the telephone with which one can beckon a doctor, and for the automobile with which one can move hastily for medicine or to a hospital. This is not to say that we expected his illness to be serious, for as parents three times over, we have been through our allot-

ment of upset stomachs and high temperatures. Nonetheless, on a bicycle trip, any single case of illness affects
everyone, putting all on the shelf until all are able to
proceed in health. In that respect, it was a little different from home where Mother is usually on hand to
nurse the walking wounded while the others go about
their normal tasks. Furthermore, we were already a week
behind schedule and any additional delay could end any
hopes we held for completing the trip to the coast.

While Chris slept, we all read. (We always carry paper-
backs whenever we travel and though space was at a
premium on the bikes, books were a great help in keeping
the kids occupied during such holdups.)

Chris awoke after about an hour's rest, still flushed,
but not as warm. He said he felt better, so after a drink
and a piece of peppermint (almost as good as Cloverine
salve), we continued. By nightfall, whatever the malady,
it had taken wings and health returned to the clan in
toto.

When we reached Terre Haute, the last outpost before the Illinois line, radio, newspaper and TV people
descended upon us en masse—our first multiple interview
city. It was also the first time we had been shot for television and our appearance on the tube that night sig-
nalled the end of any anonymity we had had. Thereafter,
no matter where we rode, people seemed to know about
the Bicycling Bauers.

After following Route 42 from below Indianapolis to
Terre Haute, enjoying relatively mild traffic, we rejoined
Route 40 again at the city on the Wabash River. What a

jolt. We reached Route 40 about six o'clock that evening and ran into a nightmare. All the truck and car traffic heading toward St. Louis explodes into two lanes at this spot, an unbelievable bottleneck, and after feeling the sucking draught of just one speeding semi-trailer, we turned tail for the shoulder and stayed there.

Inquiring around, we had been told that this stretch of highway is considered one of the most dangerous fifty miles in the country, a veritable death trap. Not wanting to add to its reputation, we sought another way to Marshall, the first city in Illinois where we hoped to stay that night. But local residents (including the state patrol) could make no suggestion, other than routes far out of our way, so we were left no choice but to ride the dirt berm for the next ten miles. Ride or walk—it was about fifty-fifty.

Not since Pennsylvania had we had such an exhausting time of it. When we weren't sashaying around deep mud ruts and loose gravel, just inches from speeding cars and trucks, their horns blasting from what seemed a mile back, we were dodging jagged beer bottles and cans that were strewn in profusion along the road. If you want to develop a genuine disgust for highway litter, try riding a bicycle across the country. The amount of trash along our roads is abominable.

With nerves ajangle, we finally made it to Marshall and a motel where we laid plans for a different strategy for the next forty miles. Under no circumstance did I intend to take the kids back out on that racetrack, even if it meant a long detour.

July 4, Thursday

Breakfasted at Marshall restaurant while clothes were washing at laundromat. During the dry cycle, I went hunting for a razor, but most all of the stores were closed for the holiday. (I had been left defenseless by the girls in the family, who in the interest of 'fastitidy,' had taken my blade a-showering and failed to return it. So, on our first day in Illinois, I appropriately wore that Lincoln look.) Before setting out from Marshall, we took time out to visit the Clark County Fair, an event well worth the pedaling.

Though I grew up in the shadow of the Williams County Fairgrounds in Ohio and am a big fair man to this day, I have not been as regular in my attendance of late as I once was. My last extravaganza was the New York World's Fair, but then one could hardly call that a fair. Why I didn't see one blue-ribbon haltered Holstein or one championship Duroc or a single trotter hitched to a racing sulky. I ask you, fair veterans, what kind of a fair is it that omits such essentials? No wonder they lost millions.

Not so, the Clark County Fair in Illinois; that fair didn't lose any millions. No siree. Inside its gates I found all the needed props for a successful fair. First, we visited the exhibit building where prize ribbons were stuck to the biggest pumpkin, the best flower arrangement, the best clutch of Indian corn, the best apple pie and the best piece of embroidery. Down the way, we ate candy apples, foot-long hot dogs, cotton candy and ice balls; rode the Ferris wheel and the merry-go-round; visited the racing barns and the stock barns. There is where one really gets the feel of a fair, the scent of a fair . . . at the barns. Chris would have stayed all day to watch the judging of sheep and cattle had we let him.

I got my fill of such competition many years before, at a fat cattle auction. Though I hail from rural Ohio, I was a town boy, and never very knowledgeable about livestock. That's why I was a little nervous when early in my late radio announcing career I was assigned to do an hour program live from a fat cattle auction showgrounds. To protect the audience from such a dude, I arranged for one of the judges to stand alongside me and answer questions during the show, expecting he would cover for my ignorance. By way of homework, I had written out three questions with which I hoped to launch the judge (who looked very authentic in a Western shirt, silky with filigree over the pockets; black string bow tie and cowboy boots) into long dialogue. However, after I came on with the usual commercial folderol, I turned to him expecting a comment of length and substance. His answer was simply, "Yup." Rifling my pockets for the questions, I shot the first one to him, something about "that heifer's confirmation."

"Fine," he said, "'cept it ain't no heifer, Son." I gulped and went on to question two, something about dewlaps. I was always interested in dewlaps because we once had a milkman with a goiter, and as a boy it fascinated me no end. Well, as could be expected, he didn't have anything to say about dewlaps, so in desperation, I turned to my last question, ready to throw the mike into a watering trough and high jump out of the ring if he didn't have something else to say but "yup."

"Would that steer probably have good marble to its meat?"

"Yup," he said, his eyes on the ground. I searched for an exit, but in the silence which followed, I heard him quietly clear his throat like the gurgle Old Faithful makes before erupting. "And," he drawled, "I'll tell you why. . . ." And that he did. For the next hour he gave that audience the best lecture on marbled meat in the history of radio. And to this day, I never cut into a piece of steak, but what I thank God for those little white lines of fat that run through the meat. They saved me from disaster.

To avoid Route 40 and its heavy traffic, we detoured south of Marshall that holiday on a county road, fully apprised by local citizenry that we were in for a dusty, bouncy ride. To add to our problems, it was in the nineties, so we had to go back to water rationing again. Even so, our two canteens were soon dry and we had to make several farmhouse stops, braving the snarls of dogs, to replenish our supply. More often than not, we were told to help ourselves to an outdoor pump.

Before our trip, I don't think I'd leaned on a pump handle for several years, but it became a regular occurrence throughout the Midwest. As nostalgic as the pump, was another piece of forgotten farmyard lore: the omnipresent community cup or tin ladle hanging nearby.

And speaking of farm lore, if you think the outdoor privy is a pillar of the past, take another look. We found and used hundreds on our jaunt. That's not to say that most farmers don't have indoor plumbing; they do, but they also have kept their half-moon stands operating for emergencies.

From our observations America seems to be adequately "johned" for conventional travelers, but it is woefully shortchanged when it comes to facilities for cyclists. Outhouses, filling stations, court houses, et cetera, are just too few and far between. So, to the credibility gap, the generation gap and the racial gap, add another gap—the latrinal gap. Though it was only a stopgap measure, our family had no alternative but to improvise as I had learned to in the Army.

Finding visual protection in trees and brush alongside the road, we often set up makeshift facilities when the situation demanded. Though legally we may not have had a leg to stand on, we assumed squatter's rights and proceeded at will. To further aid the person in the bush, we always formed a watchman's brigade. One person would be stationed at a point a hundred yards in advance, another about the same distance behind. When it was all clear at both ends, reconnaissance would give a hand signal to proceed and the person in the bush was so informed. Another signal was used to warn of approaching motorists. It was the old drill sergeant's arm pump, up and down, meaning "Double Time Ho."

Our system worked well as long as we had plenty of cover, but as we moved west foliage lessened and our difficulties increased. Our only way to compensate against open spaces was speed.

We met scores of exceptionally warm, outgoing people while we were traveling in Illinois. The afternoon we began our detour out of Marshall is a case in point.

In need of water and a place to take our lunch, we got a cordial invitation from a middle-aged couple, young grandparents, along the way between Marshall and Casey. In their front yard, we ate and talked for better than an hour while Chris napped. As it was hot and we were desperate for a cold drink, we resorted to the "Stone Soup" routine. In case you aren't familiar with the French children's story, it's about a group of soldiers returning from war. The only food they carried was a magic stone, which made soup—providing they could beg a pot, some water, some salt and a few staples—carrots, potatoes, onions, meat, etc., to give the broth a little body.

On this particular day, we had nothing but a package of Kool Aid as our stone. So first we asked for water, which the folks kindly provided. Then, we asked if they had a little ice to spare. When the woman of the house said she did, we asked if she could bring it in a large mixing bowl with a spoon, as we had no container large enough to hold two quarts. But then we discovered the drink unsweetened and, naturally, our hosts didn't want us partaking of a sour beverage, so they provided a cup of sugar.

(No cold drink ever tasted better.)

That night after we had completed the first leg of our rocky detour, we reached Casey and received more hospitality. Not finding a camping site at hand, we asked if we might pitch our tent in the town park, but a policeman said, because a carnival was holding forth there, it would be better to camp in the school yard nearby. "We patrol there during the night, so you'll be safe," he volunteered. Later, we were entertained by a Fourth of July fireworks show that the kids claimed was "the best we've ever seen."

But Casey's hospitality didn't end there. The next morning, the school custodian invited us inside to wash up before we continued and on Main Street, at a restaurant, a member of the Chamber of Commerce helped reroute us over a better road than we had planned to take.

July 5, Friday

Starting our fifth week. Now 886 miles from New York. Rode from Casey to Greenup (another pleasant, friendly community) where we were interviewed for both radio and newspapers. The radio interviewer, Doris Mitchell, an effervescent gal with a no-rundown mainspring, must have the largest audience in Illinois, for people told us about her report for days. After lunch at Greenup, we headed north on 121 to Toledo and then south to Montrose where we picked up 40 again, bringing to an end our longest detour of the trip. From here we rode to Effingham where we moteled that night. Did 41 miles, 927 for the trip.

July 6, Saturday

Made one of our best runs this morning. Rode from Effingham to Altamont, to St. Elmo to Vandalia, 32 miles on our cyclometers, in a little over three hours. At Vandalia we visited the first state capitol of Illinois, where Lincoln served with a group of legislators from Sagamon County known as the "long nine." (The combined height of the men was 54 feet). Vandalia reveres them bitter-sweetly as this group influenced the Assembly to move the capital to Springfield in 1840. After visiting the old capitol, we rode on to Greenville where city officials kindly permitted us to swim and camp at their park, though camping is generally prohibited. Mr. Paine, the caretaker, was especially helpful. Our mileage exceeded 50 for the fourth time, 55 miles for a total of 982.

July 7, Sunday

Decided to bypass St. Louis by heading west out of Greenville on 140. Reached Alton area in time for a late lunch. As we approached the metropolitan area, traffic picked up and we had a little excitement. One motorist—whether littering or aiming, I don't know—hit me on the foot with a chicken bone; another threw firecrackers out of a car window and a third reached out and slapped Steve on the back—too close for a car. In Alton, we visited a laundromat where we were interviewed for the Alton *Evening Telegraph* by Nina Meszaros, a fine reporter, who passed story and picture on to the St. Louis *Dispatch*. That account led to a wire service story and photo which was carried by newspapers, radio and TV stations across the country. While folding and packing our clean clothes, we got into conversation with a student from Southern Illinois University. It led to an interesting experience.

"My math professor, Dr. Holden, is quite a cycling enthusiast," the young man explained. "I'll bet he would love to talk with you. Would you care if I called him?"

"Well, we really must be moving along," I said.

"But, he only lives down the street," he persisted. Finally, I agreed to say hello to his esteemed professor, figuring he must be an unusual man to have made such an impression on this student.

About five minutes later, Lyman Holden and his wife, Martha, showed up. Their charm was hypnotic and inside five minutes, they had convinced us we could do nothing else until we had come to their house for refreshments while Chris slept. Though we planned to stay only an hour, it ballooned to over two, and it was nearly five o'clock before we could bring ourselves to leave. But they had more service to render.

Because of the heavy traffic across the Mississippi River bridge at Alton, Lyman believed it would be easier if he followed me over the span in his car, to sort of run interference from the rear. The move proved a wise one, for with the Holdens shadowing us we could ride two abreast on the two-lane bridge and the traffic was kept off our backs. When we reached the other side and pulled off the road, autos streamed by Lyman as if he were the pace car at a big race.

There, just a few yards into Missouri, we said goodby to the Holdens, watching them turn around and head back into Illinois. We did not expect to travel over that bridge again, at least right away, but we were mistaken.

15 No Missouri Waltz

Heading out Route 94 which follows the Missouri River, we figured to make as good time in the Show Me State as we had in Indiana and Illinois. I had lived in Missouri (at Lebanon) as a boy while Dad had been stationed at Fort Leonard Wood during World War II and therefore knew a little about the terrain. I had plotted a line I thought far enough north to avoid the roll of the Ozarks, but map reading was never one of my best skills in either the Boy Scouts or the Army, and our dead-center route across the state turned out to be a 300-mile roller coaster.

The trip from Alton to St. Charles, north of St. Louis, was an exception. It was tabletop level. The rocky road we remember was purely analogous.

We were still patting ourselves on the backs for having ridden Indiana and Illinois in one week, 159 and 181 miles respectively, or 340 for seven days, 1,030 for the trip, when Shirley made a nerve-rattling discovery: her purse was missing! In addition to the million and one items all women's purses contain, hers also held a dozen or so credit cards, several hundreds of dollars in traveler's checks, a personal checkbook, our car and house keys, all clearly addressed, and nearly all the cash we had along. I think I had $13.54 plus one New York City subway token in my pants pocket.

A search through the bicycle baskets produced nothing, so we mentally retraced our movements. Was it at the restaurant outside of Alton, at the Holdens, the laundromat . . . ?

"Yes, the landromat," Shirley said. "I had it beside my chair in the reading room while the clothes were washing. I must have left it there."

Up the way, a Volkswagen bus loaded with Daddy, Mama and kids was pulling out of a driveway. I flagged them down and explained our problem. The driver, Chick Presley, a salesman, parked the car and he and his pretty wife, Peggy, led me inside to their phone where I made a series of calls. The laundromat had no phone, so I dialed the Holdens. Martha said she would go back to the shop and make a check.

While I was waiting for her return call, Chick fixed

me a drink and we chatted about their home, his work, their family. (Not all the kids I had seen in the car belonged to them, I learned. Some were foster children. "We have served as foster parents for about a dozen kids over the years," Chick explained.)

The phone rang. Martha had gone to the laundromat, but the attendant was not there. Neither was the purse. Furthermore, there was no answer when she dialed the business' emergency number, but she volunteered to keep trying. I told her I would call later, realizing the Presleys were going away, but they insisted they were in no hurry. Next, I phoned the Alton police station. When the desk sergeant answered I barely got my name out before he interrupted me: "Yes, Mr. Bauer, we've been expecting your call. . . ." He had the purse; everything was intact. "Bring Mrs. Bauer in to identify it and it's yours."

The news was more than either Shirley or I had expected. If even the credit cards had shown up, we would have been relieved. The traveler's checks could have been stopped and the money written off. But this was too good. Chick Presley drove us back to Alton, via the Mississippi bridge that we had ridden only an hour before, and at the police station Shirley collected her pocketbook, putting some money in an envelope for the women who turned it in—an Alice Garner, according to my notes.

"You have some wonderful people in Alton," she told the desk sergeant.

"We got all kinds," he answered. "Over there on the board are some of the others." He pointed to a cork bulletin board and a collection of "wanted" posters. Off to one side was one which had been retired. It was the mug shot, description and fingerprints of James Earl Ray, the man accused of shooting Martin Luther King.

"He boarded with us for a while," the sergeant said. "Yes, we got all kinds in Alton."

By the time we got back to the Presleys, it was nearing seven o'clock. Only a couple of hours remained until darkness and we had over twenty miles to ride to St. Charles with no communities to speak of in between. I explained the situation to the kids and we set out at a wicked pace, buoyed by our good fortune with Shirley's purse. We made excellent time, but when nine o'clock rolled around and the last sliver of light had disappeared on the horizon, we were still nearly five miles short of our destination. A back route had given us some freedom from traffic, but as we neared St. Charles we came out on the main highway again. It was jammed, heavy with trailer-pulling cars returning from vacations.

As outside Terre Haute, we went to the shoulder to ride, but we had an additional handicap, darkness. Turning on all our lights, we walked and rode the last three miles in constant fear one of us was going to hit a broken bottle and blow a tire. We did have a mishap: a broken caliper which left Shirley without front brakes. Other than that we arrived beat, but whole, at a hotel in St. Charles where we munched half-heartedly on hamburgers and sipped listlessly at milkshakes, really too tired to eat. And no wonder: we had come 67 miles, our record for a single day.

July 8, Monday

After breakfast, we wheeled the bikes out of the hotel lobby where the desk clerk had allowed us to park them and rode to a bicycle shop. The proprietor was too busy to help much, so I tried my hand at installing a new caliper brake on Shirley's bike. My first try resulted in failure; I had placed the spring in backwards. The second effort was successful, but it was 11 o'clock by then. The delay sent us off into the heat part of the day, and it was a boiler. Also, the road was narrow and hilly and traffic was heavy. Less than ten miles up the way, we pulled off for lunch and Chris' nap. We didn't get started again until nearly 3:30. Past Weldon Springs, we had some memorable excitement . . .

Dogs and bicycles just aren't the best of friends. Those flashing spokes and churning feet of the cyclist must be about as magnetic as a soup bone because at times, man's best friend wasn't. To avoid being bitten, the procedure is to raise your feet up under your chin and pray that the dog goes away before the bike coasts to a stop. In Missouri, we seemed to have more trouble with dogs than anywhere else. Though some cyclists carry a spray such as postmen have been known to use, we battled the dogs Clyde Beattie style.

I remember we had just fought off a pack of three German shepherds, all growling and gnashing their teeth, when we came upon a young black poodle, who took up the challenge and gave chase. Now there is considerable difference in jousting with one dog and three. With only one canine in pursuit, it is a simple matter to lift one's leg on the side he is attacking. However, when three dogs are nipping at your sneakers and you are surrounded, you must turn circus performer and pull up both legs, preferably resting them on the handlebars.

After prepping against the German shepherds, the poodle was no match at all, and Steve and I left him in the dust. Shirley and Laraine, who were half a hill and a bend in the road behind us, got his full attention. But before the dog reached them, he ran into trouble or vice versa. The alarm was a long, drawn-out squeal of brakes, and we turned just in time to see Blackie go underneath a car, a flopping ragamuffin. I knew he had had it.

At the bottom of the hill, Steve and I got our bikes stopped and turned around. Though I wasn't anticipating the sight that would greet us at the top of the hill, we went back. What came into view as we reached the crest is unforgettable, comic on one hand, tragic on the other. There in the middle of the highway standing over the fallen ball of black fluff stood traffic cop Shirley, her arms extended defiantly in both directions, demanding that traffic halt. Being on a hill and a curve, it is a wonder she wasn't hit, but her guardian angel was about, for cars and trucks—and there were many—all ground to a stop.

When we reached the spot, the dog's mistress had come to the roadside, but stood frozen in shock.

"Come and get the dog," pleaded Shirley, still holding the traffic at bay.

"I . . . I'll have to get my shoes," said the woman, and while the traffic continued to build, the woman walked back to her front door and disappeared inside the house. By the time she came out again, there was a chorus of horns asking what was the delay.

Meantime, the dog, apparently knocked unconscious, was coming to, and by the time his now-sandaled mistress reached him, he was sitting up. Carefully, the woman moved him to the yard where we all examined his injuries. There was no blood anywhere around his head or mouth, a good sign, and only one apparent wound, a cut on one hind leg. Nonetheless, the woman agreed with us that the dog should be taken to a vet. As we rode off, she had regained her composure enough to thank Shirley for her help, as well she might, for had not my frau risked life and limb, the kayoed dog would no doubt have been run over by another car. And, face it, one miracle a day is about the limit for anyone.

At the village of Defiance, we stopped for the night, camping behind a grocery store. Though there was a shortage of grass to soften our lie, that was not the most annoying drawback about our tent site. Not by a long shot. The store owner forgot to tell us we were camping right next to a railroad track, and we didn't see it as we prepared for sleep in the fading light. But we learned about it in the middle of the night when a long freight passed within twenty yards of our tent.

The way the earth shook beneath our sleeping bags and the way the front tent pole jitterbugged, I thought

How Many Hills to Hillsboro?

it was a quake and jumped outside to investigate. Standing there in my underwear, I saw the swirling light of an engine coming toward me.

"It's all right," I said through the parted tent flap, "it's only an iron horse."

"A horse!" exclaimed Shirley, thrashing in her sleeping bag.

Thank heavens, we were not on a main line. It was the only train to pass through that night.

July 9, Tuesday

We started this day 44 miles deep into Missouri—20 from Alton to St. Charles and 24 from there to Defiance. Between Defiance and Augusta, the next town, we hit some of the most rolling roads we had seen since Pennsylvania. Several times we had to dismount and walk, but at Augusta we were directed to Washington via a bottom-land road along the Missouri River. Though the road was level, it was freshly tarred and our bikes were a mess by the time we crossed the river into Washington. We stayed the night on the south side of the river at New Haven. Incidentally, we seemed to be winning a battle with poison ivy that infected a couple of us, but the chiggers were gaining. Turpentine, the local remedy, was refused in favor of a druggist prescription, which worked. Surprisingly, ticks were no problem on the trip.

July 10, Wednesday

Though I had tried to remove the fine grit and tar from our chains and *dérailleurs* with gasoline and an air compressor, the bikes needed a more thorough cleaning. My bike in particular squeaked for attention; something was askew in the back wheel. At Hermann, I discovered the problem. Or rather friendly Joe Kruegel did. Joe, a transplant from Kirkwood where he was in the bike business, told me several of the bearings in my back wheel had been ground to powder. He dropped his other work and helped us service all the bikes. Though it took several hours to make the necessary repairs and service, the time was worth it. Joe, incidentally, refused to charge us. It was nearly four o'clock when we left Hermann, crossed the river to 94 and set off for Portland, but we had a flat just after Rhineland. To compound the problem, my portable air pump blew out, so I had to hitchhike back to Rhineland to have the tire repaired. A newspaper deliveryman out of Jefferson City who was traveling in the opposite direction, stopped, turned around, took me into town, waited while the tire was fixed and then returned me. Quite a good turn I would say. We finally made Portland by nightfall, camping on the banks of the Missouri and eating at a bar where I thought I was going to have a catfish dinner, a big favorite of mine, but the creel was empty. Our mileage that day, 30, following 32 the day before, brought our trip total to 1,136.

July 11, Thursday

More tire trouble. More fine stones and tar. And more ungraded hills. Reached the capital, Jefferson City, about two P.M. Then, pedaled to a Schwinn shop where we cleaned out the grit again. A malfunction of Steve's *dérailleur* went unrepaired, however, despite all kinds of coaxing. Owner gave me a new

> *dérailleur* to put on if I could not get it adjusted.
> Stayed in Jefferson City that night. 34 miles, 1,170.

July 12, Friday

> Switched to Route 50 and rode to Tipton in time for
> lunch, despite two more flat tires. Tried to buy new
> tires there, but out of stock. By the time Chris had
> had his nap, it was nearly five o'clock and storm
> clouds carried by a heavy wind had moved in . . .

We were in a quandary. On one hand, we did not want
to quit for the day with only 31 miles under our belts; on
the other, if we continued we would most likely get
drenched or blown off the road. The memory of the
tornado in Ohio was still fresh in our minds and the
wind was building.

A vote was taken and we decided to chance it, though
the fierce blow that lashed us the first three miles, made
us wonder if we had made the right move. Then it began
raining hard. We stopped long enough to get into rain
gear, but rode on. The rain, coupled with the wind, made
miserable riding so we decided to sit it out under the
shelter of a service station canopy at Syracuse. In less
than five minutes the rain stopped and we took to the
road again, riding through deep puddles that splashed
our legs and feet. It didn't matter, however; our feet
were as wet as they could get.

Earlier in the day, a state patrolman had suggested
that we might want to camp that night at a park near
Otterville, but when we reached this spot, we were mov-

ing at such a good clip, we decided to try for Sedalia, another twelve miles. We made it by 8:15, covering the twenty-six miles from Tipton in a little more than three hours. Our gamble paid off, as we added fifty-seven miles that day (1,227 total), our first good day in stubborn Missouri.

The next morning we visited Mr. Cecil's Schwinn shop where he and his son helped change all our tires. Though our tires were not worn out, they showed some cuts and we had lost considerable time because of flats, so we put on all new rubber. While the work was being done, men from the Sedalia radio stations and the newspaper showed up for interviews. One of them questioned the children and Laraine and Steve surprised me with their poise and confidence before a mike. Chris had something to say, too.

On our way into Sedalia the night before, we had passed a huge turkey farm—a segregated farm with white turkeys on one side of the road, black turkeys on the other. But it had rained on both sides and the turkeys were complaining loudly. Apparently, all the gobbling and wing-flapping had made an impression on Chris.

"How do you like the trip, Christopher," queried the announcer.

"The turkeys are all wet," he answered in a non sequitur to top all non sequiturs. I forget the announcer's comeback, but he didn't ask Chris any more questions.

Shirley had a show to herself. Invited out to one of the stations to appear on a homemaker's program, she gave the woman's angle on cycling, including a little history of women's attire from bloomers, which were designed for gals on bikes back at the turn of the century, to pedalpushers, to culottes—the outfits she and Laraine wore most of the time.

After more hospitality from the Cecils, we rode out of town, me with a bottle of stomach medicine in my back pocket. I had become the second health casualty on the trip, but like Chris my upset tummy lasted only a few hours.

More upsetting was a steel grating in a gutter that I hit on the west edge of Sedalia. Though bicycle groups all over the country have campaigned against wide-spaced drainage grating, many towns still have not replaced these traps. Fortunately, I was not traveling fast when my front wheel fell part way through this one, but it stopped the bike with a jolt and gave me quite a scare. People have been thrown from their bikes and killed as a result of such accidents.

July 13, Saturday

> Now in our fifth week, we covered 30 miles this half-day of riding, 1,257 total. Still about 250 behind schedule and we are not making as good time in Missouri as hoped. Stayed near Warrensburg for the night and ate at a combination tavern-night club-pizza parlor-discotheque . . .

When we asked a motorist about the pizza up the way, he flinched.

"It's all right, isn't it," I said, meaning the pizza.

"Oh, yes, the pizza's fine," but there was reservation in his voice. I figured it was the idea of taking children into a tavern, but we had done this often on the trip—out of necessity in many cases, out of recommendation of the food in others.

At the doorway, a young man was taking tickets— $1.50 a piece as I recall. Well, I've paid some steep cover charges, but $7.50 for a pizza was a little more than I intended to shell out.

"May we come in for some pizza?" I asked.

"You don't want to dance . . ." he began. Then, looking down at three-foot-two Christopher, he continued, ". . . no, you don't want to dance. Well, if you have your pizza and come right out, I won't charge you."

We proceeded. Just inside the door, a psychedelic light swirled menacingly in our faces, blinding us to the darkness which followed. Led to a booth, we had a seat and waited to place our order. In the interim, we watched miniskirted gals stroll by in twos and threes, followed by groups of young men who often took separate tables— at least until they learned the girls' names. In a world at sea in change, it was reassuring to see that this game is still played by the same rules.

But what followed, I hesitate to describe, for fear of being called a cube. By way of preface, let me say I don't dislike rock music or whatever they're calling it these days, but I do not care to have my eardrums broken. That is why I was a little worried when five or six musicians up in front cranked up their amplifiers and tried to blow me out of the place. From the expression of the ticket taker's face I knew that we were not their usual clientele, but this was ridiculous. Had there been another restaurant nearby, I might have taken the hint, but we were tired, we wanted a pizza and we wanted to go to bed.

We finally ordered our pizza, but I had to write the order on a napkin, it was that noisy. While we were waiting for them to bake, Shirley and I held our ears to lessen the pain. But we were the only people out of it; everyone else was swinging all over the place. Even our kids. Laraine was bobbing up and down in her seat, Steve was pounding on the table with his spoon and Chris was doing a modified twist, standing up in the booth.

I have since read that such racket can, in fact, damage one's hearing, and after this night I have no doubts of it at all. Whether it was over the 120-decibel trouble point or not is immaterial. I only know that our pizza arrived in the nick of time. Otherwise, I would have gone to bed hungry. On the positive side the pizza was great, though I've never eaten one so fast in my life.

July 14, Sunday

From Warrensburg, we rode to Lonejack where we turned off on 150 in order to bypass Kansas City proper. Outside Greenwood, Bob Neal of the Kansas City *Star* intercepted us for an interview. "I've been looking for you for hours," Neal told us when he pulled up in his car. "Even the state patrol has lost you." When I asked if they were trying to get in touch, fearing some emergency, he advised that they had been keeping tab on us all across the state.

"We've had daily reports as to your whereabouts," he said. A few minutes later, a state patrolman wheeled up, gathered some information for a report, then drove off. We thanked him for their surveillance. After the newspaper and a KCMO-TV interview, we headed for Martin City, on the Kansas-Missouri line. It was getting late and we made a sustained drive to reach the community where we expected to find a motel. We had been misinformed . . .

Arriving at nightfall, we scanned the area for a place to stay, but found nothing. I didn't like the feel of things. At one house on a large lot, I stopped to ask if we might camp in the side yard. A woman listened to my request and was sympathetic, but said she would need to phone her landlord. I waited on the porch in the dark. In a minute she came back. "No, I'm sorry, but he says not to let you. You understand . . . we've had lots of problems around Kansas City—murders and robberies and. . . ."

I thanked her and walked back to Shirley and the kids. "What do we do now?" I asked. For once everyone was silent.

16 The End of the Line?

Leaving Shirley with the kids on the main route, I walked down a poorly lit side street in search of a tent site, a flashlight in hand. I knocked at a couple of houses where lights were burning inside, but no one came to the door. So I ventured further down the gravel road, the sound of my shuffling feet reminding me of the weariness I had forgotten when I learned the community motel-less.

There is something a little scarey about being in a strange town at night without a place to stay. And even though we had been through this bit many times before on the trip, it still caused the adrenalin in my system to run faster. I don't think I would make much of a hobo. Though we hadn't resorted to a jail for shelter so far, I thought this might be the night. Not everyone knows it, but a police station is always a shelter possibility for stranded travelers.

At the next house I came to, on the left-hand side of the street, I saw people inside, apparently watching TV. One step on the porch roused the occupants and a young man came quickly to the door. He was a good-looking chap with blond hair and a friendly demeanor. I repeated my story, the same one that had failed a few minutes before. The only addition was: "We would have made it here before dark had we not been held up by newspaper and television people."

His face brightened. "Oh yes, I think I heard about you on radio. Sure, you can pitch your tent in our back yard." After we had set up camp, we left to eat at a restaurant we'd passed a couple of blocks back. When we returned, the young man and his wife, Jerry and Marty Dickey, came out to tell us some news.

"We saw you on TV. You were on for several minutes."

Then, Jerry had an admission to make: "There has been a lot of mayhem around Kansas City recently, so I decided to check you out. After you left, I called the TV station and asked if they had interviewed you. They told me to watch the news show and we would see for ourselves. Also, they were glad to know your location. A cameraman may be out in the morning to take some more pictures." (Shirley groaned under her breath in anticipation of another delay.)

A little while later, after we had all climbed into our sleeping bags and the kids were asleep, Shirley and I— lying on our backs half inside, half outside the tent— talked as we studied the sky, an opened jewelry box of fiery diamonds thrown against luxurious navy blue velvet. The subject of our conversation was what politicians were calling the "fear in the streets" issue. Before our trip, we assessed much of this talk about widespread fear as over-statement, but it was more real than we had imagined. Real like a shadow is real, though. Twice this night it had come up as we tried to find a place to stay, and it had also been threaded through many other conversa-tions along the way.

"What are people afraid of?" Shirley asked.

"Each other," I yawned.

"Isn't it more the haves being afraid of the have nots?"

"It's not that simple."

"I think it is," she persisted. "It's the racial problem. The violence it has created is what fear-obsessed people are worried about."

"Mostly, I suppose, but if that's true, most of it is planted fear. I haven't talked to anyone on the trip who has had any confrontation with violence, unless looking at a riot on TV is direct confrontation."

(The thought reminded me of a conversation I'd had with a Midwest friend a summer before. He'd cancelled a trip to New York City after seeing a newscast showing the trouble in Newark. He was amazed to hear that I continued to ride a train through Newark, commuting into New York. It was about the same reaction that another out-of-city acquaintance had when he learned that I occasionally visited the Lower East Side and Harlem. I serve on a committee of businessmen which works with and supports a fantastically successful group of street workers. They belong to an organization called *Young Life* and their mission is to help young people, especially Negro and Puerto Rican school dropouts.)

"Then, you're saying," Shirley translated, "that our highly developed communications system is responsible for most of the fear that people have?"

"Hardly. You can't hang slums and poverty and bigotry and ignorance and prejudice and injustice on the news media. Those are people problems that create tensions, that explode into violence, that make news, that is reported and that sends fear rippling across the country like a stone tossed into a pond."

"An endless cycle," she mused. "Where will it stop?"

"When we start to make a significant dent in the root causes of these problems, helping people to help themselves out of their predicaments and at the same time protecting the population from the destroyers, those who want to tear everything down in order to pull themselves up."

"You think that will cause this fear that people harbor to disappear?" Shirley asked, pulling her sleeping bag up around her neck and edging back inside the tent.

"No, but it will help. Then, maybe we can begin to move the other way and start to build up trust in each other again."

Shirley was quiet for a minute, then had another

thought: "You know, people who are suspicious and mistrusting seem to invite trouble to themselves. They seem to be accident prone."

I reminded her that the Bible says as a man *thinketh in his heart, so is he.* "Scientists say that dogs can tell when men are afraid by the odors they give off. Humans sense this in each other by some kind of vibrations. For example, parents can pass on their phobias—fear of storms, death, disease, germs, etc., to their kids without ever stating those fears. . . ."

"What fears are we passing on to ours?" she mumbled, rolling over, a signal that she had had enough discussion.

"Nothing that affects their sleep, apparently." I fumbled for the flashlight and turned it on. At the end of the tent Chris, hemmed in by duffel bags, was resting contentedly. Across the front of the tent, lined up like felled poplars were the rest of us: Steve buried so far down in his bag that he was out of sight; sun-tanned Laraine, now a few months short of high school, lying in a beauty pose—arms akimbo like the gals in the mattress ads; and Shirley, off to dreamland, her feet snuggled under my sleeping bag in search of warmth. The temperature of her feet has not varied much in fifteen years of marriage. They are approximately forty-two degrees year around.

It was exactly six thirty when I stepped out of the tent next morning, thinking we'd get an early start and be gone before our hosts were up. But while I was still stretching, Jerry Dickey, who is a construction worker and therefore an early riser, called out the back door, "The coffee's hot and the bacon and eggs are cooking."

And they were. Protesting didn't do any good; the Dickeys were determined to feed us and we were grateful for the hot breakfast. It was going on eight when we rode out of their driveway, out to the main highway and off toward the Kansas line just a few minutes away. When we reached it, I checked my cyclometer. It told me that our route across Missouri had measured 289 miles. Our seven-day trip from Alton brought our total to 1,319 miles.

July 15, Monday

> Rode from Martin City to Olathe, Kansas, then took Route 56, which roughly follows the old Sante Fe Trail, southwest toward Gardner. Wind, stiff, so stiff in fact that we were weighing an early lunch stop. On the east edge of Gardner, we got a surprise . . .

The press coverage from the Kansas City news media further stimulated interest in our venture, and more and more people let us know they recognized us by honking their horns, waving and shouting their salutations. Many stopped their cars along the road and waited for us to arrive, wanting to shake our hands and talk; but when such delays started interfering with our mileage, we tried to make our chats as brief as possible without seeming rude.

Outside Gardner, two men waited near their car, apparently to get a better look at us. I instructed the others to keep riding.

"Howdy," I said, raising one hand in a modified gentleman's wave.

"Could we see you for a minute?" the older of the two asked.

"We're running a little late . . ." I answered, pedaling by.

"I'm the Mayor of Gardner . . . and we'd like you to join us for lunch. . . ." he called after me.

That stopped me and we did dine with the mayor, the editor of the town paper and several Gardner businessmen. Actually, the mayor was detained in his office—babysitting with Christopher, who had inopportunely dozed off. Hizzoner graciously volunteered to stay with him at City Hall while the rest of us lunched. (As a reporter I have seen my share of baby-kissing politicians, but this was my first encounter with a baby-sitting mayor. Definitely above and beyond the call.) After lunch, we returned to City Hall where we collected Christopher and a key to the city, a memento of our visit to this friendly community, portent of Kansas-type conviviality to come.

July 15, Monday

> . . . After Gardner, we rode on to Baldwin where we had a swim, compliments of the Chamber of Commerce, and another interview. Made 37 miles, 1,357 total.

> Wind out of the southwest gusting to 35 miles an
> hour blew in our faces all day. Made Overbrook (20
> miles) by noon, thoroughly exhausted. Swam and
> rested most of the afternoon. Made another try about
> 4:30, but 10 miles up the way at Scranton we called
> it off. The stores were closed and our larder was near
> empty, so we searched for a place to eat. A good
> many of the storefronts were boarded up—casualties
> of a decline in railroad jobs, we were told. About the
> only choice for dinner seemed to be Gert's . . .

Now Gert's is not the name of the tavern where we
dined that evening, but Gert was the gal who ran the
place (and I assumed owned it). When I say "ran it" I
mean she was 100 percent in charge.

Gert and one other helper were taking orders, filling
them, serving them, cleaning up, doing the dishes and
handling the cash register. Though there seemed to be a
good deal of commotion coming from the men—a couple
of dozen of them—who sat at the counter, Gert was not
about to be rattled by anything, least of all impatient
customers. We sat at a table opposite the bar and waited
our turn, not expecting much of a dinner. Gert had given
a nod in our direction so I knew that she knew we were
there. Meanwhile, we entertained ourselves by reading
the numerous signs on the wall behind the counter. You
know the kind: "If you drive your husband to drink,
please drive him here," and "Credit kindly refused."

After a while one of the boys at the counter became
inquisitive: "Are you the folks who are riding to Cali-

fornia?" (He'd apparently seen our bikes out front.) We told him we were and more questions followed from others at the bar, who swiveled around in their seats and chatted. Before long, almost all the stools were turned our way as if we were the floor show.

Finally, Gert came over to our table, wiping her hands on her apron. She reminded me of my grandmother, tall though more slightly built, but her gray hair was swept away from her face in much the same manner. And her eyes showed a similar strength of character.

"Whatcha' have, folks?" she asked in a deep voice that reminded me of Lauren Bacall.

"What's on the menu, Gert?"

"Try me," she snapped.

"Sandwiches . . . hamburgers?" I said, half to her, half to the kids. She nodded approval.

"Potatoes—fried?"

"Sure thing."

"A vegetable?"

"Maybe I can dig up a can of green beans back there."

"Milk and coffee."

"Okay." And off Gert went to prepare what I imagined was the most elaborate meal that she had fixed since the last Eastern dudes passed through her emporium. We read more signs. One said emphatically: "No one allowed behind the counter." I read it again to make sure it didn't say "anyone" because there seemed to be a steady stream of customers helping themselves to another cup of coffee, a glass, silverware—all behind the counter.

In a few minutes, Gert delivered the goods, served

family style, and when we had finished, she left the bar trade long enough to inquire if we were full.

"What about you, Honeybunch?" she grinned, chucking Chris under the chin. It was the first time I'd seen her smile, but it was enough to tell me that beneath her generally stern facade there was a twenty-four-carat ticker.

When we asked Gert where she would recommend we pitch a tent, she directed us to the town park. "I'll tell the marshal you're there," she said. "He can keep an eye on you, make sure you're okay."

Later that night, in the park, the wind which had been brutal all day, picked up in velocity and brought with it heavy rain which battered the tent until we thought it might come down. But the next morning, it was still standing, though we had taken some water, and the bags and some clothes were wet. The wind was still growling, too, and spitting rain.

"We can't ride in this," said Shirley, as she pulled on a sweater. I had to agree. Dark clouds overhead were angry and roily, apparently ready to drop more rain. So we rolled up the tent, packed the bikes under a nearby shelter and returned to Gert's.

She was standing in the same place I'd last seen her, bent over a work table, her back to the counter. I thought to myself that possibly she'd spent the night there. When she turned around and saw us sitting at the bar, she gave us smile number two, a big smile for Gert.

"How'd you sleep?" she asked on her way to the cash register.

"Fine."

"Get wet?"

"A little."

"Well, you need some breakfast to warm you up." Once again, Gert fixed us a huge meal that was not on the menu—a large bowl of scrambled eggs, a couple of dozen strips of bacon, toast and jelly, milk and coffee. After everyone was finished, I walked to the front door and looked out. The rain had stopped, the wind was down and the sun was shining. It was hard to believe.

"Let's get started," shouted Steve.

"First, let me pay for our breakfast," I said. "How much do we owe you, Gert?"

She frowned, squinted, looked at the ceiling and then asked: "Would two dollars be about right?"

"No, it wouldn't," I answered, "you're robbing yourself."

She laughed. "No, that'll be plenty." She handed me my change and said, "Thanks for stopping in. Take care of that Honeybunch."

The thanks were ours to give, but Gert just waved me away and went back to her work table.

Thank God for the Gerts in this world.

July 17, Tuesday

From Scranton, we rode to Burlingame, bypassed Peterton and headed for Miller. We had finally reached the wide open spaces. Outside Miller I left the clan to rest while I searched for a grocery. Returning with rations, we ate on the bank of a river and then unrolled our wet tent and bags, leaving them to dry in the sun while we slept. Pedaled to Allen for supper and considered camping there, but decided instead to make a run for Council Grove, 16 miles away. We reached that old cattle-driving center as night fell.

Few experiences from the trip are more vivid than the ride we made into Council Grove. Entering the fabled Flint Hills, world-renowned for their lush pastureland, we marveled as the setting sun played kaleidoscope with the rolling countryside which was liberally laced with grazing cattle. The landscape turned from a verdant green hue to dozens of shades of purple, while the sun went from a wheel of cheese to a Temple orange to a carnation. As night came, we reached a bluff looking down on the city which was coming awake with lights.

It was not hard to imagine how inviting the scene must have been over the years to pioneers and cowboys, who came upon it tired and dirty after a long day on the trail. It was an oasis in the desert. Inspired, despite our fatigue from fifty miles of riding, we covered the last three or four miles in near record time, arriving at a motel on the east edge of town about nine thirty.

And having no horses to water, we went straight to bed.

July 18, Thursday

Interviewed by Council Grove newspaper after breakfast and laundry stops. Though wind had diminished, the irrepressible Kansas heat bore down on us as we made the 23-mile ride to Herrington before lunch. Too hot to continue, we found a swimming pool.

After a detour, we headed for Marion, but were forced to take cover at Lincolnville when a short, but heavy storm hit. It cooled things off, however, and we rode with new resolve to Marion, arriving about eight o'clock. A total of 55 miles, 1,504 over-all —more than halfway to the coast at the end of six weeks.

July 19, Friday

Before we pulled out of Marion, we had three news-paper interviews and on the way to McPherson, 35 miles away, we passed through another Hillsboro where we held still another session with the press. At McPherson, I called New York and learned that several other people were trying to reach us for inter-views. I initiated a couple of calls (one to Sharon Bertsch, a talented writer for the Trenton *Times*), but we were approaching the saturation point and had to make a choice: either to ride or to conduct interviews.

I might at this point make a comment about the news reports of our trip. For the most part stories about us were factual, well-presented accounts, but a few bordered on fiction—putting me on the defensive with my kids. As a former newspaperman, I always have maintained that the press is amazingly accurate considering the amount of news it handles, and I still contend this. However, Laraine and Steve found some isolated cases which re-butted this claim and they gave me the third degree. Several reports took liberty with our statements and put words in our mouths that had never been there. With this practice, I take issue. On the human error side: our residence was reported as New York City; Princeton, N.Y.; Princeton, Maryland; and Princeton, Virginia. Gremlins were also busy playing with my age. At the beginning of the trip, most reported me to be thirty-four. Correct. But then, thirty-two, thirty, twenty-nine. By the time we reached Kansas, I had aged to forty-three (a transposition which appeared in the New York *Daily News* and possibly other papers).

After a swim in McPherson, a flat tire, a broken gear cable and a visit to a Schwinn shop, we set out for Lyons, passing through or by such tourist attractions as Conway, Windom, Little River and Mitchell. All of these places were, I believe, crowned by one common landmark, a grain elevator. As we moved across Kansas and through wheat country, the landscape became more and more barren, giving an open canvas to these concrete towers. From our bicycles, riding under a scorching sun, it often seemed they were playing games with us, edging a yard back for every yard we came forward. Like racing with the moon, it seemed we weren't gaining.

Despite all the time we spent with the press, we tied our record this day, riding into Lyons at nine thirty, completing a 68-mile day, for a 1,572-mile total.

July 20, Saturday

"Oh, no," complained the kids as we got on the bikes this morning. The wind was high again. By struggling all morning and part of the afternoon, we made it to Great Bend, but not without great physical and mental exertion. Our hopes for making it to the coast are beginning to look dim. We had figured to pick up lost time in Kansas for sure, but we are at the mercy of the prevailing winds, often directly in our faces or just to the left or southwest a bit.

Another cyclist, Ken Moore of Redding, California, caught up with us in this attractively modern community. Together we posed for newspapers and TV. Ken, a college student, was on his way home after a trip from California to Missouri. I queried him about his experience in riding through the desert and the Rockies, taking notes for future reference if we made a shot at them. His principal advantages were far less baggage and a 15-speed racing bike which enabled him to cover 100 miles and more with ease in a day.

After Ken went on his way we visited the zoo at Great Bend, resting until evening in hopes the wind would die, but it didn't. On the west edge of town, I called the weather bureau at Dodge City and asked when we could expect the wind to moderate. "Buddy," the meteorologist told me, "you're in Kansas." His suggestion was to ride at daybreak. So we parked the bikes at a motel (34 miles for the day, 1,606 total) and planned an early takeoff . . .

We rolled out of bed at four fifteen, ate a makeshift breakfast, packed the bikes and began riding at five fifteen. It was still pitch dark and the wind was blowing just as hard as when we went to bed. Steve and Laraine were most discouraged, so I tried to divert their focus. "Take a look back every so often and check the sky. Sunrises are often as pretty as sunsets. Keep your eyes open— never know what you might see." Just then a falling star

179

streaked across the sky, and the sky held their interest until daybreak.

We reached Larned, covering twenty-three miles, in time for a second breakfast, then set out for Garfield, which we captured shortly before noon. There we rested.

By staying with Route 56 at Larned, we had committed ourselves to the southerly route to California. At Larned, 156 led off toward Pueblo, Denver and San Francisco. Reporters had by now begun asking us how we were going to travel through the arid desertlands of the Southwest. I answered that we would cross that bridge later. Ken Moore had made it on speed. By moving through the desert in a hurry, he had avoided getting hung up between stops without shelter or water. (He had resorted to sleeping in gas stations on occasion, he told me.) We lacked speed, so would need another strategy.

My plan was to hire an escort jeep, which we would light up forward and back. By riding early enough and late enough, I figured we could make it in short takes. When it became too hot, we would stow the bikes in the jeep and seek cover. Later in the day, we would have the driver return us to our interruption point and continue. What worried me even more was the Rockies. I wasn't sure we had enough intestinal fortitude to battle the heights again. And, of course, these grades would be much worse than Pennsylvania. (Young Ken Moore told me, I believe, that he walked his bike only twice in the Rockies, but we couldn't expect to match that record with our five-speed gears.

July 22, Monday

> Drained from the previous day's heat, we were dis-
> heartened by the news which came over the transistor
> radio as we rode out of Kinsley. The weather report
> called for temperatures near 100 and winds gusting
> to 35 miles an hour. Battling every inch of the way,
> we managed the 20 miles from Kinsley to Spearville
> by 11:30, where we decided to eat. When we came
> out to our bikes at noon, the heat was nearly un-
> bearable. Ride or take cover? We studied the map;
> Dodge City was just 17 miles up the road. If we could
> make it there, we'd pull in for the day. We decided
> to try, a big mistake.

The trip from Spearville to Wright, about eight miles,
was the toughest eight-mile straightaway of the entire trip.
Excruciating. Water didn't help; rest didn't help; and
there were no trees to seek cover under. The further we
moved away from Spearville, the more inviting became
the shade created by an occasional trestle for the railroad
tracks which ran alongside the highway. Only the thought
of a sleeping copperhead or rattler off there in the brush
kept us on the bikes.

Finally, we reached Wright and an air-conditioned
restaurant. We lolled there for better than an hour, satis-
fying our thirst which was enormous. Though we tried to
limit our intake of liquids, knowing that it would work
against us when we went back to the bikes, the tempta-
tion was too great. We also took salt pills to compensate
for the water our systems were pouring out.

At the restaurant, I called into town and made a reservation at a motel, instructing the owner that we would probably be in after sundown. We had been told there was a rest area, a mile up the road, so we rode there. It was the last resort. If we had ridden any farther I know one of us, maybe more, would have passed out.

Under one of the rib-roofed shelters, we rested. It was too hot to sleep, but we closed our eyes. After a while, we played Rook and listened to the radio to pass the time. A newscaster announced the temperature at 102 degrees at four o'clock. A short time later, he reported a tornado, twenty miles north, moving in our direction. We were in a totally open area should it have chosen to set down there, and Laraine, ever the optimist, reminded us that Dorothy in the *Wizard of Oz* had gone into orbit from Kansas.

We decided not to move (unless moved by a tornado) until the temperature came down. It didn't budge much in the next hour or the next. I think it was still 98 at six o'clock, when we decided to make another run for it. The last nine miles were a repetition of the torture we had experienced before, and the wind was still blasting our arms and faces with hot needles. We fought for yardage like a football team. I remember that we stopped at a cattle overlook about three miles from Dodge and weren't sure we could go on.

"Don't forget, there's a swimming pool at the motel," I told the kids. They licked the salt water from their upper lips and doggedly went back to work. I had to smile at their determination. They had grown in many ways in the last few weeks.

It took us almost two hours to ride the last leg into Dodge City and, when we finally reached the motel, we were so limp we could barely walk. I got the key, let the others into the room and returned to register. When I came back, I found Shirley draped across the bed in a fashion that reminded me of our early conditioning days in April.

Slumping down in a chair with a glass of water, I told her: "I've had it. We're quitting."

17 Oh, Those Lovable Sooners

After a refreshing swim and a huge dinner, we gathered again back at our motel room. A newspaperman was trying to reach us, but I didn't want to talk with him until I had talked with the kids about calling off the trip at Dodge City. In Ohio, just after we had come out of Pennsylvania, I had told the troupe we would continue riding as long as it was fun. Though the last few days of riding had not been unrewarding, they had been tough going.

"We are nearing 1,700 miles," I told them, "but even

with a break in the wind, we will still be between 200 to 300 miles short of where we should be come Thursday night." (The end of our seventh week.) "Because our chances of making it all the way look slim, you may want to call it off here, ship the bikes home and go by train to the coast."

Steve and Laraine offered reasons for both positions . . . on one hand . . . on the other. . . .

"What's the weather forecast for tomorrow?" asked Steve. I dialed the number from a pad I kept in my shirt pocket. By now, the meteorologist and I were getting well acquainted. He told me it would be more of the same tomorrow—hot and windy. When I reported this to the kids, they moaned. Then, Shirley had a recommendation: "We are all tired tonight and the prospects of riding tomorrow are not very appealing. What say we take a day off and think it over. Maybe we can make a unanimous decision tomorrow night after we've looked over the sights of Dodge City." Everyone cheered that idea, and so it was that we took our first break since Laraine's mishap, thirty-six days prior.

I returned the newsman's call and tried to hedge about our trip plans, but the story went out on the wire that we had been stymied by the Kansas heat, and some I understand, took this to mean that we were quitting.

However, it was amazing what a day in Matt Dillon's old bailiwick did for our spirits. The highlights were a visit to Boot Hill and the Long Branch Saloon where we met all the "Gunsmoke" cast, portrayed by local residents, and drank ice-cold sarsaparilla (root beer with a gunpowder chaser, I believe). Incidentally, the evening floor show is highly recommended for the entire family. All good fun. One of the more memorable and characteristic lines in the skit was this observation on feminine pulchritude: "Beauty may only run skin deep, but homely runs clean to the bone."

That night I called the weather bureau once again and they had encouraging news for the next day. It was all we needed to nudge us on.

July 24, Wednesday

TV cameraman showed up at the motel and shot us riding away at five A.M. After breakfast, we left for Sublette, 50 miles away. The wind was down, so we zipped through the dark at a good clip. Later, when the sun would normally begin taking its toll, a cloud cover gave us cooler than normal riding. Past the grain elevator landmarks we sped—Ensign, Montezuma, Copeland, Tice. Shortly before noon, we arrived in Sublette, 50 miles in one morning—a new record. After lunch, we rested and then hit the trail again about five o'clock. Our next town was Hugoton, though we doubted we could make it that night. We underestimated ourselves. Four hours later, we arrived, completing an 87-mile day, our all-time high. Total is now 1,780 miles.

July 25, Thursday

Our motel hosts, Fred and Gene Hinsch, took us to breakfast before we went on our way to Elkhart. At the restaurant we had a newspaper interview and a

visit with an old friend of former mile run record
holder Glenn Cunningham.

I had hoped to visit Glenn's ranch outside Augusta on
our way through Kansas, but our route took us too far
north. Not long ago, I did a story about his rehabilitation
work with troubled young people—a story that is the kind
I like to write. It not only recounted Glenn's comeback
from a tragic fire that took his brother's life and left him
temporarily crippled at the age of twelve, but told of the
miracles he and his wife have wrought through their
ranch which has seen over 8,000 boys and girls come and
go in the last twenty years. Though the Cunninghams
have spent all of their savings and have gone into debt
to continue this work, I can truthfully say they are about
the richest people I ever have known. I'm sorry Shirley
and the kids didn't get to meet them.

Again, we had wind to contend with, so we pulled off
the road after thirty-five miles at Elkhart, on the Kansas-
Oklahoma line.

Our cyclometers recorded 495 miles of Kansas riding,
bringing our total for the trip to 1,814. It had taken us
eleven days—ten of riding—to cross the Sunflower state,
making our average almost fifty miles a day. We had
finally reached the goal we had set for ourselves at the
beginning, but there was some question in my mind as
to whether we could maintain the pace as we moved
farther west.

At Elkhart, we surveyed the route ahead. A new concern: the long stretches between towns. We had added another canteen, bringing our water-carrying arsenal to three quarts, but it wouldn't be enough in this heat.

The first and only place of any size that we would pass through on Route 56 in the Oklahoma Panhandle was Boise City, over forty miles away. The next town after that, another forty miles, was Clayton, past the northwest tip of Texas, into New Mexico. After that, I thought I had a map of the moon.

July 26, Friday

> Got up before daybreak and rode in the darkness into Oklahoma against a wind that must have been blowing 35 miles an hour. Laraine complained of a soft rear tire, but I told her it was the wind which was making pumping difficult. However, at daybreak, I saw that she was right . . .

We were about halfway between Elkhart and Keyes, the next town before Boise City. As my portable tire pump was on the fritz, I had two choices: find a compressor at a ranch (and that might not be easy, especially at six A.M.) or hitchhike into town. Since traffic was sparse, I decided to try at a farm house.

After two failures along the highway, Laraine and I rode inland a half mile to try another house. Dogs greeted us as we came near, but they were called off by an elderly woman who stood in the doorway of her house, buttoning a faded housedress.

"Do you have an air compressor? We have a flat on one of our bicycles," I shouted.

"I dunno', I'll ask my husband."

She disappeared inside. Then, through one of the open windows, I saw a white-haired man roll over in bed and come to a sitting position on the edge. Up went one leg as he struggled into his trousers, then the other. Two out of two. Standing up, he completed the job, whipping suspenders over his shoulders and zipping his pants. In another minute, he ambled out the front door, running his hands through already rumpled hair. In addition to his pants, he wore a gray sweatshirt which he had apparently been sleeping in, but no shoes.

"Howdy," he said. "What can I do for you?"

"My pump is broken and I need some air to fix a flat on my daughter's bike."

"I've got butane on the truck," he answered, pointing to a pickup standing nearby.

"Swell." I took the tire off and patched it while he and his wife watched. Then, he walked into the barn and came out with an old tire pump, left over from the Model T days.

"Could you use something like this?"

"I've refused two of them on the trip because of space limitations, but if you want to sell it I'll be glad to take it along."

"Don't wanta sell it, I want to give it."

My acceptance sealed a friendship which up to that time had been tenuous. After that we got into a long-winded conversation about his forebears. His pappy had

come from Illinois to Soonerland and he had lived on the
farm for a "coon's age." After the bike tire was repaired,
I sent Laraine on her way and turned to leave myself,
shaking hands with each of them. The wife, who hadn't
said a thing since she greeted me from the doorway, was
poised to speak . . .

"Are you the folks who'er goin' across country?"

"We're the ones."

She smiled self-consciously. "I just thought you're the
ones."

At Keyes, twenty-six miles into the famed Cimarron
Strip, we made a refreshment stop, and there noticed
my back tire going flat. It was a slow leak which I
couldn't find so I changed tubes. Setting out for Boise
City about one o'clock, we tried every trick we knew to
beat the wind, but nothing helped. Every hundred yards
or so we stopped to rest. Though Boise City is only
seventeen miles it looked like an all-day pedal. That is,
until the Boise City Chamber of Commerce, represented
by Norma Gene Young, editor of the Boise City *News*,
showed up.

"We'd like you to be our guests for lunch," said Norma
Gene in a burst of Sooner hospitality that was hard to
refuse. We decided we could return and ride the bikes
on into town that evening, so we took the Boise City
businessmen up on their offer and a panel truck was sent
back for our bikes. After lunch, we were taken to a motel,
compliments of the Chamber of Commerce, furnished
with a car and given a historical review of the area by
Roy Butterbaugh, Norma Gene's father and the editor

emeritus, who had survived the Dust Bowl days. Mr. Butterbaugh told me that the paper would have gone under in the late thirties had it not been for some sheriff sale ads which law says must be published.

"Most of these real estate sales were for pieces of property that had been deserted by people who'd given up and moved on. To pay the taxes, they were sold at sheriff's auction. The revenue from those ads saved our necks."

Another man told me his memories of those days as a child: "It seemed that every day about nine A.M., the wind would come up, bringing with it a curtain of dust that made it impossible to see across the street. My mother would hang wet sheets at the doors and the windows and then take us to the basement where we would play and she would sew until evening." There were other stories of perseverance all told with a subtle pride by indomitable people who had fought an uphill battle and won. No wonder some of them burn with such patriotic fervor. Their stake in America has been only recently assured.

That night, we returned by truck to the spot at which we had been rescued, and rode our bicycles to the motel with relative ease. The head wind which had so impeded our progress that afternoon had moderated to little more than a zephyr, and with the better part of our load closeted at the motel, it was pleasant indeed.

When we reached Boise City for the second time that day, Norma Gene was waiting on us with her children.

"Want to come down to the house tonight?" she asked,

leaning out the car window. "We'll make some popcorn."

We accepted the invitation and that evening her husband, Bob, came by the motel and drove us to their place. Our visit that evening with the Youngs is another of those not-to-be-forgotten experiences.

Like the Swopes in Indiana, the Youngs are "now" people, excited about life and its possibilities. They were, we found, particularly in love with their part of the country. Sitting in the Oklahoma Panhandle, Boise City is less than an hour's drive to four states—Kansas, Texas, New Mexico and Colorado—and all the outdoor pleasures these states afford.

One of the Youngs' favorite vacation spots, we learned, is the art community of Taos, New Mexico—a direction in which they often head for weekend skiing. Their dream is to build a winter retreat on a wilderness site they have purchased in that vicinity.

Once again, we stayed longer than early-rising cyclists should, but it was a night when time seemed to lose its importance. We made a tentative date to go skiing with Bob and Norma some time in the future, and I look forward to seeing them again. Wonderful folks, a wonderful town!

18 Roped by the Cisco Kid

July 27, Saturday

Left Boise City for Clayton, New Mexico, at eight A.M., rode the 43 miles with only one stop, but it was a gruelling trip. We had refreshments and took on more water at a community called Felt, and later were treated to Cokes by a banker and his wife who stopped us on the highway to say they had seen us on TV in California; another family shared ice with us at a picnic spot on the New Mexico line.

Our benefactors at the roadside park were from Liberal, Kansas, on the Texas line. We had originally thought of riding Route 54 through Liberal, Guymon, Oklahoma, and Dalhart, Texas, on our way to Tucumcari, New Mexico, but decided that Route 56 offered more oases.

The decision nearly caused us to miss Texas entirely—an intolerable occurrence for Steve and Laraine. We would have bypassed it inadvertently had not Norma Gene Young apprised us of a survey marker that sat just to the south of Route 56, a couple of miles after we entered New Mexico.

Steve, riding out in front, had to be waved back to the marker in order to join the rest of us in a fifty-foot detour off the road, around the barrel-like marker (which noted on a plaque that this was the northwestern-most point of the state of Texas) and back onto the highway again.

It was comparable to a little boy sticking his big toe in a tub of water and then claiming to have taken his Saturday night bath, but the maneuver satisfied the kids, who now informed Shirley and me that we had ridden in 12 states, four—Kansas, Oklahoma, New Mexico and Texas —in the last two days.

We reached Clayton at three o'clock, minutes before a big storm hit. Though the drag on the bikes told us we were on a climb, it was fairly gradual. The more awesome evidence was on the horizon ahead.

"Wow, are those big mountains!" exclaimed Steve.

Again, we were the guests of the Chamber of Commerce, which provided us with both food and lodging. One thing about this southwestern hospitality: our expenses were sure falling off!

July 28, Sunday

> Because Springer, New Mexico, lay 80 miles away over difficult terrain, I knew we could not execute the run in a single day, so I called ahead to make motel reservations and to arrange for a pickup about half way. We would have to cycle it in two installments . . .

The day was hot and the hills oppressive. Furthermore, the climbs were growing progressively longer. Not far out of Clayton, we began to flag, and I knew the end was near. True, we were only in the shadow of the Rockies, but already the thought of what was coming began to intimidate us.

When we began to walk some of the hills again, our negativism built. (*If we can't make these, how are we going to get through the Rockies?* is the way our minds started working.) We had three choices at Springer: north through the art center of Taos, which promised miles of uphill walking; or south through Glorieta Pass, also plenty of uphill walking; or—and this was our growing inclination—we could ride the train.

The decision came casually and in a hurry. About one-thirty we pulled off the highway for lunch and parked our bikes in a treeless driveway, which apparently led to a ranch house at the foot of the next mesa. As we ate, we talked about the obstacles that stood in our way between here and the coast. The predominant one was time. We could not make it in the ten weeks we had allotted, and as I had to be back in New York the middle of

How Many Hills to Hillsboro?

August, it was only a question of stopping now or later.

"At the rate we're moving, we aren't going to come near our rendezvous point and I'm afraid our driver from Springer may turn around before he finds us," I began.

"Maybe you should stop at a ranch and try to call him," Shirley suggested.

"I doubt if we'd get any answer."

"We could try to hitch another ride," Shirley said.

What she was saying was, "Let's scrub the trip."

"You mean, call it quits?" I said, asking for a clarification.

"Well, we have come 2,000 miles. Don't you think that's a good point to kind of . . . ah, retire?" She was avoiding the word *quit* and when I posed the proposition to the kids I did the same.

"I'm sure we could make it if we could add a couple of weeks to the schedule, but you'll have to ride it without me. Sorry, but I've got no more time."

That was the magic twist—it was because of Dad that we had to stop. Suddenly, all were in agreement. We pulled off to the side of the road and I stuck up a thumb. In about five minutes, we got a bite.

Chugging to a stop was the most decrepit blue pickup truck I have ever seen. Its paint was faded and peeling and one fender was hanging by a couple of bolts. Still, we weren't demanding anything fancy and we had no hesitation about accepting a lift from these folks—a man and his wife.

Out of the cab crawled a wizened Mexican-American ranch hand, whom I would judge to be at least seventy

198

years old. He wore the uniform of a cowboy—a blue denim shirt, levis, boots and a well-turned ten-gallon hat. Smiling, he waited for me to speak.

"We need a lift. We are trying to meet another pickup about twenty miles up the road." He mumbled something in Spanish, obviously not understanding. Unfolding the map I carried in my basket, I pointed to a spot on the map. He studied it, then pointed to a spot short of mine.

"Fine. Okay. We ride with you there," I said.

This was clear, because he joined in helping me load the bikes into the back of the truck. Actually, there wasn't any room to load them *into* the truck, we just stacked them *onto* the truck. It was crowded. The man and his wife had apparently been to town on their weekly shopping trip as there were several boxes of groceries in the truck. Also, there was a horse saddle with lariat around the horn, several boards, a tin box of tools and to top it all off, an unfriendly black and white mutt, terrier background. When we started to pile the bikes into the back of the pickup, the dog got out. Unfortunately, the saddle couldn't walk. But once all our gear was loaded, Shirley and Chris climbed inside the cab with the man's wife while Laraine, Steve and I took seats in the vacant space behind. Seats were about as plentiful as Democrats at a Lincoln Day buffalo roast.

The driver stood back and studied the load: it didn't satisfy him. Reaching into the truck, he took his lariat and walked a short distance away. Suddenly, he began twirling it overhead like the Cisco Kid. When he had the loop wide enough, he let fly, throwing it over the whole truck—the cab, bicycles, us, everything. Then he tied a couple of fast half hitches and got into the truck.

"Will Batman get here in time to save us?" I called to the kids.

After a revving up, the truck gave a lurch and we were off—almost.

"Whoa," I called out.

The truck jolted to a stop.

"Si?" the man said, peering down at me from the front running board.

"Your dog, bow-wow, woof-woof," I said, trying to raise my arms from under the bikes and rope. "He's back there in the middle of the road." We had forgotten Fido and I believe he would have been quite content to walk home. Yet, when the man called the pooch's name, he reported—not pronto, but he came. He was less coopera-tive when his master tried to lift him into the truck. Putting his paws on the edge of the tailgate, the dog at-tempted to resist, but it was no use. Resignedly, he draped himself over my feet and closed his eyes.

Though the dog wasn't happy about our being aboard, we were.

19 God Bless You, America

Fifteen miles up the road at a spot where a dusty path forked north, the driver edged his pickup off the highway and brought it to a squeaking stop.

"This is where they turn," Shirley informed those of us in the "back seat" as she climbed out of the cab. After we were untied and the bikes unloaded, there began an extended round of goodbys, lengthened by our difficulty with each other's tongue. We smiled and nodded appreciatively. They smiled back, shook our hands vigorously and bowed low. I returned each bow, emulating

the Japanese and Chinese actors in World War II vintage
films. (The only variation was that I didn't say "ah so" or
"so sorray.")

I did indulge in a little linguistic razzle-dazzle, however. When "thank you for the ride" brought a response
of "Si, thank you," I decided to lay a "grazie, paesano"
on them, causing more puzzlement. Then, I realized
that I was drawing on my twelve-word Italian memory
bank instead of my sixteen-word Spanish portfolio.
Spanish for thank you, I suddenly remembered, is
gracias, but I couldn't for the life of me recall the word
for friend or brother. What I needed was a pony like the
one that carried me through Latin I and II. Or maybe in
this case a pinto.

What was it that Tonto always said to the Lone
Ranger, I asked myself. Suddenly, it came back as I
mentally hummed the "William Tell Overture" . . .
"Adios, amigos."

"Gracias, señor," and "Adios, amigos" I said, enunciat-
ing each syllable as if he were deaf.

"Adios, amigos," he replied, grabbing my hand again
and squeezing. Now I was hot. In a flash, I recalled a
couple of words from a visit to Puerto Rico . . . "and
buenas noches, señora," I said to his wife. Then, I quickly
corrected myself, "Ah, buenos dias,"—it was only three
o'clock.

The woman, as wrinkled and worn as her husband, and
as charming, passed among us distributing kisses and
abrazos. Finally, we pulled ourselves away and pedaled
up the road, waving as we went.

A hundred yards removed, I turned halfway around on my seat to make one last mental photograph of the scene: the faded blue pickup . . . the dog (which now reminded me of the old RCA mascot, Nipper) resting in the shade of the fender about to fall off . . . the man in cowboy hat, holding his lariat . . . and his wife, clutching her shawl in one hand, waving tirelessly with the other.

We ran onto our lift from Springer a half an hour later, but not any too soon. The sky was a churning inferno of black, preamble to a storm, and we scrambled hurriedly into our second truck—a new one this time.

Once the bikes were strapped in place, and Steve and I situated in the bed again, with Shirley, Laraine and Christopher in the cab, our driver, Joe, a man of about forty I'd guess, set out for Springer. We weren't en route more than five minutes when the storm hit, buffeting Steve and me about something fierce.

Joe stopped the truck for a minute to see if we were okay.

"Sorry, I don't have a tarp," he shouted, squinting up his bronzed Indian features.

"We're all right. Keep going," I called out from under the poncho I had pulled from my bike basket and wrapped tentlike around Steve and myself. Joe went back to the wheel and drove on, causing the wind and rain to whip in on us once more.

Steve took one corner of the poncho, I the other, and we huddled closely against the sideboards, warming ourselves on each other in mutual dependency. I remembered a fatherly squeeze I had attempted to give him not long prior; he had refused it with an embarrassed look which said, "Get off it, Dad, I'm a big boy." But there was no withdrawal now as he unashamedly nestled under my arm.

"Do you want to come back out here tomorrow and try to ride this?" I asked, just after the pickup reached the top of a steep grade. Shivering, Steve shook his head from side to side and answered, emphatically, "No, Sir. I'm ready for a train."

No question about it, the bicycle part of the trip was over.

At a motel in Springer, Joe, who proved to be an entertaining conversationalist—filled with Southwestern legend and lore—blanched noticeably when I tried to pay him for his trip.

"No, you don't owe me nothin'," he insisted. "My favor."

"Well, at least let me pay you for the gas."

He wasn't sure, but I finally stuffed a ten in his hand and he accepted, though he tried to give me change. Before he left, he asked if he could bring his wife by to see us.

"By all means," I said, "we'd like to meet her." He promised to drop in after supper, "if she's not too tired."

But bedtime came and still no Joe, so we turned in, a little sorry. I wondered if I had said something to make him think it was an imposition.

The next morning, we rose early and rode our bikes a few blocks to the Santa Fe depot to await the day's only passenger train south to Albuquerque. It was due about seven A.M., as I recall. Since the ticket office was closed, we were a little worried that they might not accept the bikes as baggage, but there was no difficulty in that regard. Our problem came when we attempted to lift the bikes into the baggage car.

Vainly, I hoisted mine—fifty pounds without Chris— toward the car bed while the man on board held onto a handgrip and leaned out as far as he could, but we missed connecting by about a foot. On the second thrust the gap was further. Then, I mustered all my strength and heaved. As I did, something behind me suddenly supplied an extra boost and the bike literally flew into the car. Turning around, I stood face to face with Joe.

"What are you doing here, Joe?" I asked.

"Just wanted to say goodby," he shrugged.

"All aboard," the conductor called. Quickly Joe and I lifted the other three bikes into the baggage car and Shirley climbed aboard with the kids.

"Joe, you're a godsend. Thanks for everything."

"Let's go, fellow," prodded the conductor.

I broke away and jumped on board. As the train began to move out, Joe walked alongside: "Come back and see me some time."

"Will do," I shouted back through cupped hands. Then, just as the old couple had done the day before, Joe, too, began to wave and was still waving the last glimpse we got of him. Another addition to our gallery of unforgettable people.

On the way to Albuquerque, I opened the log and scratched in some final figures. We had come from New York to Springer, New Mexico, almost two thousand miles on the nose, in less than eight weeks. Taking into account the two days we were sidelined by Laraine's spill, the day we sat out in Dodge City and the several half days we missed because of bike maintenance or repairs, I figured we averaged close to forty-five miles a day.

After arriving in charming Albuquerque, I made a few phone calls to inform the press that we had officially ended our bicycle assault on America, two thirds of the way across.

"Why did you quit?" one reporter asked over the phone.

"Quit?" I answered, feigning offense. "We didn't quit. We made a decision of discretion." Neither Laraine nor Steve, who were reading across the room, looked up, but I knew they were listening.

"How's that?" he asked, a little impatient with my gobbledygook.

"Well, if you mean why did we decide to finish our trip by train, I'd say there were several contributing factors. For one, the rattlesnakes."

"Rattlesnakes? You mean while you were camping?"

"No, riding. They kept biting holes in our tires." There was a guffaw at the other end.

"And along the same line, these jack rabbits crossed

with antelopes—'jackalopes,' I think you call them—kept knocking us off our bikes." The kids were by now enjoying the horseplay.

"But the most serious problem was your tree disease."

"Tree disease?" he asked incredulously.

"Yes, starting in southwest Kansas it has just about wiped out all the trees. I tried carrying a cottonwood for two or three days so Chris would have some shade to nap under, but the tree was too heavy and we had to drop it."

When we finally got serious, I listed these reasons as the ones which led us to punt:

1. We were running out of time. I had to be back in New York by the middle of August and it would have taken us at least until September first to make California, leaving no time for our appointment at Disneyland.

2. The heat was getting to us.

3. We had no stomach for walking any more mountains. Our mental and physical reserves for hiking had been worn to a frazzle.

4. Riding west, the wind is a nightmare. The next time we try a coast-to-coast bike trip, we will start in California and wear coats with batwing sleeves. (We will also carry less weight and ride ten-speed bikes.)

There were a couple of other formalities to finish off before we could mark our bike trip completed. We had to turn our wheels over to a Schwinn dealer who agreed to crate them and ship them home; we had to mail our equipment, choose some different clothing and buy some suitcases to replace our waterproof duffel bags, which by now were as holey as colanders.

After a night in Albuquerque's historic Old Town, we left for the Grand Canyon, and other stops on the regular tourist circuit, in style. I had gone in search of luggage that afternoon and found some bargain pieces at a little shop not far from our motel. The store had three brass balls dangling from a sign above the entrance. Over enchiladas and tacos that evening, I mentioned my good fortune on the three pieces of matched luggage and both Steve and Laraine wanted to know more about the workings of a pawn shop. (I regretted not having taken them with me; every kid should visit a pawn shop—a most practical lesson in economics.)

The following morning at the Albuquerque railroad station, Steve and I were standing in a long line of dignified-looking people, waiting to check our new luggage when he picked up the trend of the conversation again. In a voice audible throughout the waiting room, he said:

"Considering they came from a pawn shop, Dad, these suitcases aren't bad."

After Albuquerque, we visited the Grand Canyon (arriving late at night and getting just one brief pre-breakfast peek at it before rain and fog set in) and Las Vegas (where the kids marvelled at the grandeur of the neon lights and the town's preoccupation with religion—wall-to-wall wedding chapels) and finally Los Angeles.

When we arrived on the coast, we went directly to Disneyland where, for two days, Shirley and I attempted to match strides with our bubbling kids. At times, we longed for our bikes. However, it is a magnificent attraction—enjoyable to all ages. After two days, though, we were ready to head back into town, intending to show the kids the many sights of L.A. It didn't work out that way.

Shirley was packing our bags and we were preparing to check out of the Disneyland hotel, when Chris asked a most precocious question:

"Are we going home, Mommy?"

"Not yet," she answered, drawing him to her. A vacuum-like silence followed. Then, Laraine spoke.

"When *are* we going home?"

"Are you ready?" I asked. She pursed her lips and with one hand on her hip gave me a noncommittal shrug. "I guess I could be talked into it."

"Steve?"

"Yes, any time."

I didn't have to ask Shirley. She talks with her eyes. Walking to the telephone, I called the airport and asked: "What is your first plane to New York?"

"There's a flight at 3:25 . . . how many people, Mr. Bauer?"

"Five."

"Just one minute." Laraine and Steve sat down on the bed, their chins in their hands. I studied my watch. We still had to check out and catch a bus into town. It would be close, but we should be able to make it.

"Mr. Bauer," the reservations' clerk continued, "we can confirm space for five on United flight . . ."

"Please book us on it," I said.

A big cheer went up behind me—the homesick were going home.

Four hours later, we were on our way east, covering the country from 31,000 feet at 610 miles an hour—a differential of at least 600 miles an hour from the way we traveled it coming out.

On my side of the aisle sat Laraine and Steve; on the other, Shirley and Chris. All wore going-home smiles on their heavily suntanned faces. No question about it, the trip had been good for us in many ways, but I wanted to hear from each his evaluation of the experience while it was still fresh.

Shirley, ever the mother, thought it was a successful venture because it brought us closer together as a family. Each one had to contribute or else we got nowhere.

"Less bickering, more teamwork than on other vacations," was her assessment.

I would have asked Christopher his opinion, but figured he was a little young to be articulate. Anyway, I had a fairly good idea of what he thought. He had come through the trip in fine shape—without any mishaps and only one day of minor sickness—and, for the most part, had enjoyed the excursion, especially when there were animals or machinery to see. (The unending string of oil wells in Kansas with their methodical putt-putt pumps were of great fascination to him.)

The major annoyance for him I believe was confinement to one place: the seat on the back of my bike. Six or seven hours a day in that position was no doubt tiring at times for a tot used to relatively free rein at home. To compensate for this, we tried to make regular stops for refreshments and recreation and he was always ready to run about with his brother and sister while Shirley and I flopped under a tree to rest. Without fail, we set aside a substantial swath of time out of the hot part of the day for Chris to nap and play. He needed a little unwinding period before he was ready to rest and Shirley often read to him during this time. Since he was a baby, he has enjoyed having someone read to him and Shirley kept renewing his book supply enroute.

Before we set out on the trip, we were concerned about his welfare, more so than anyone else's, but there was never any question about taking him or leaving him behind with the grandparents. That has never been our philosophy in raising children. Shirley, in particular, has strong feelings about including everyone in family activities, and in this case I know she would have voted to forget the trip rather than leave Chris out. It has always been that way.

When Chris was just five weeks old, he went along with the rest of us on a 6,000-mile camping trip to Yellowstone and back. A year later, he was included on a 4,000-mile camping trip through New England, Nova Scotia and Canada, and the year before the bike trip, when he was two, he had gone along on a seven-country tour of Europe. How well we remember celebrating Steve and Chris' day-apart birthdays, picnicking outside a little French town south of Paris. The birthday cakes were chocolate cupcakes punctuated with candles—which I recall were difficult to light because of the wind.

In all of these experiences and others before them, we always have fared marvelously well with the children, and never have we felt it a mistake to take them along. Shirley, an experienced child psychologist without formal credentials, reasons young children may not remember the details of such experiences, but that they will remember the feeling of being included and loved. She further maintains that this base makes for a secure, self-confident person later on.

Looking across the aisle of the airplane at Christopher handling his own shrimp cocktail seemed evidence enough that she knows whereof she speaks.

When I turned to Steve, he noted that the trip was "fun, but lots of work."

"But was it worth the effort?"

"Sure." Then, after a pause he added, "Nobody else I know my age has ever ridden a bike that far." Once again, the element of pride had come to the surface. A little of which is proper and understandable, for boys need a few such conquests to prove their masculinity.

I was also interested in his mention of the word *work*. The trip had extracted more physical energy from all of us than we were used to expending, but this is one of the pluses of cycling, one of the reasons the physical fitness people are so high on it as a conditioning method.

Watching the kids respond to the challenges we had to face—the weather, the terrain, fatigue, pain; the minor deprivations of going without water at times, eating foods that would be turned down at the table, missing a little sleep—revealed to me some gratifying character traits that highly automated twentieth century living doesn't normally show. For as we moved along, I observed them toughening up, physically and mentally, excelling, competing, maturing.

Finally, I turned to Laraine for her thoughts. What seemed to impress her most was people's interest in us, concern about us, goodness to us.

"A few months ago, we were talking about the future of America and you indicated a big concern about some of her problems," I began. "What do you think of her now?"

"Well, the people were kinder, more wonderful than I expected. . . . They treated us great."

"Then you didn't observe any violent or hate-filled people?"

"No, but . . ."

"But what?"

"But maybe they wouldn't treat somebody else as well as they did us."

"What do you mean?"

"Well, I wonder how we would have been treated if we were black?"

"What do you think?"

"I'm not sure," she hedged. "Most of the people we met would be nice to anyone, I'd think, but then some wouldn't, I guess."

"So what do you conclude?"

"What was the sentence Anne Frank wrote in her diary?" she asked ponderingly. Then answering herself: "In spite of everything, I think people really are good at heart."

Her simple wisdom shook me, as do many of the insights that come from young people today. Though some adults choose to dwell on this generation's long hair, loud music, bizarre clothes, protests against the Establishment, morals, e.g., preoccupation with sex, I cannot help but score most of the current crop high on honesty and integrity. Also, I buy their idealism and order of priorities. The Peace Corps' success is evidence of their good visceral instincts. I sympathize with the young men and women who feel that "dropping out is the solution to today's complexities, I cannot endorse it as responsible, positive behavior. I think many already have seen the light. But then, I'm an optimist: I have unqualified faith in the younger generation, faith that it will, in the last analysis, do the right thing. Just as I have faith in America. We will emerge wiser and stronger from the plethora of problems that now bind and confuse, disunite and diffuse. One could not travel across this land of ours and see what we did, feel what we did, without coming to this conclusion.

Somewhere over Pennsylvania (the hills are easier at 31,000 feet), I pulled out a pad and began jotting down the chores that faced me once I got home. There were bills to pay, an expired driver's license to renew, a magazine article deadline to meet, a book to finish, a conference to attend, some house painting to do, a church meeting to arrange, letters to write. . . .

As the list hit the bottom of the page and spilled over on the other side, I began to feel something building inside me, a sensation that comes when the fantasy world from which vacations are spun starts breaking up. Part of this feeling is a pressure we all experience; it's related to responsibility, involvement, commitment. Part of it is anticipation of the opportunities, the challenges, the excitement which lie ahead. Like a racehorse pawing at the starting gate, I was getting ready to break from the chute.

As the plane banked to make its approach at Newark, I got a brief look at the New York skyline and the harbor with the Statue of Liberty still beckoning ". . . your tired, your poor, your huddled masses yearning to breathe free. . . ."

Ten weeks earlier we had sailed past Miss Liberty about to go in search of a country we had begun to doubt and mistrust. Now, we were returning, transfused with new hope and new faith drawn from the veins of her incomparable sons.

We had found the real America—the one that had been there all the time.